SWIFT Act

Swift Action for Permanent Recovery

For information about permission to reproduce selections from this book, write to
SWIFT Act Alliance, 1900 W Chandler Blvd, STE 15-285, Chandler, AZ 85224.
Email: info@swiftact.com

Cover design by Shon Quannie
Website: www.4x-media.com

ISBN: 978-1530583188

Library of Congress Control Number: 2016904582
CreateSpace Independent Publishing Platform, North Charleston, SC

SWIFT Act - Contents

Figures and Illustrations

Forward

This book is published as a companion volume to *Wall Street, Trade, and the New Economy*.

SWIFT Act provides a summary indictment of the New Economy, and also presents specific proposals to transform the American economy.

In the four years it has taken to write these books, there has been an unmistakable continuity of policy that perpetuates the status quo.

The Federal Reserve has committed enormous resources to buy toxic mortgages from Wall Street banks, *at the rate of $75 billion a month in 2013, followed by an additional $30 billion a month in 2014.*

If that amount of money had been invested in manufacturing, the impact would have transformed the economy.

Instead, the Fed serves the Wall Street economy, by promoting *asset inflation* in stock and house prices, instead of promoting manufacturing and the revival of American industry.

The banks that in 2008 were too big to fail, are 30 percent bigger today than they were then.

The 2015 budget deal overturned a key provision of the Dodd Frank financial reform, so now derivatives are backed by federal deposit insurance.

The budget deal makes a mockery of Dodd-Frank, while senate reform bills to break up the banks die in committee.

Meanwhile the administration and majorities in both houses of Congress support a new "NAFTA for the Pacific," otherwise known as the Trans-Pacific Partnership (TPP).

Like NAFTA and similar trade deals with Columbia, Panama, and South Korea, TPP is just another word for offshoring.

Offshoring is not trade.

"Trade" describes selling things made in America to other countries, and vice versa.

Offshoring involves shutting down American factories, re-building those factories overseas, and selling the products back into the American market.

Thanks to offshoring, the U.S. economy has been stripped of productive capacity and can no longer create enough jobs.

At the same time, our politicians seem blind to the reality that *banks are not factories*.

An economy based on manufacturing employs a large work force, while an economy based on finance can't generate enough jobs.

Preface

There are two inter-related problems.

Offshoring is not trade;
Banks are not factories.

Since the 1980s, the decline of manufacturing and the rise of finance have created an economy that can't generate enough jobs.

With consumers in debt and incomes stagnant, we spend over $1 trillion dollars a year on imports from low wage countries.

Spending on imports drives growth offshore, instead of driving growth in the U.S. economy.

Three decades of stagnant wages spent on low wage imports have reduced *demand for domestic goods* to a point that it no longer justifies private sector investment.

This is the fundamental problem of the economy today.

Meanwhile the Obama administration and the Federal Reserve remain committed to ongoing stimulus for consumption, augmented by propping up real estate values in the housing market.

Political power is in the hands of those who ignore the danger posed by
- deflation in the real economy, and
- another financial collapse on Wall Street.

This reality of our politics is seen in the bipartisan 2015 budget agreement that includes federal deposit insurance for derivatives.

SWIFT Act outlines five key areas of reform as follows.

Smart Growth – understanding the problem requires acknowledging that GDP growth based on inflated asset values in stock and house prices is not what we need.

What we see instead is the opposite of smart.

The stock market is posting record highs, while the Federal Reserve inflates the housing market by purchasing toxic assets from Wall Street banks.

Wage Standards – imports from low wage countries are the Achilles heel in the New Economy.

Wage growth is limited because American industry can't compete with U.S. multinationals that offshore production.

The problem isn't going away.

We can impose wage standards on imports, or we can live with the consequences of stagnation.

1

Industrial Policy – the private sector sees levels of consumer demand that don't justify the investments needed for recovery.

Strategic investments in manufacturing, funded by the federal government, will be required for permanent recovery.

Financial Reform – imperatives for reform include breaking up the banks and repealing the decision in Citizens United that allows unlimited and undisclosed contributions to political campaigns.

Levying taxes on the financial sector would also serve to reduce the profit advantage currently held by finance over industry.

At the same time, taxes on the financial sector could be used to generate revenue to fund strategic investments in manufacturing.

Trade & Tax Reform – the adoption of a value added tax (VAT) would serve to rectify the trade disadvantage we have with 150 countries around the world that use a VAT.

Adopting a VAT would also generate revenue that could be used to fund strategic investments in manufacturing.

A VAT would make exports more profitable and imports less profitable.

The effect would be to create incentive for investment in manufacturing, and disincentive for offshoring.

How hard is that?

If you're not the recipient of Wall Street contributions to your political campaign, my hope is that you'll agree it's a no brainer.

The name SWIFT Act also embodies a symbolic message.

SWIFT is an acronym for the Society for Worldwide Interbank Financial Telecommunication.

SWIFT handles financial messaging between member banks and financial institutions engaged in international transactions.

Among these is the Bank of International Settlements (BIS), an international organization owned by central bank members in sixty countries.

Here's how academic historian Carroll Quigley describes the BIS: *"The Power of financial capitalism had a far reaching plan, nothing less than to create a world system of financial control in private hands able to dominate the political system of each country and the economy of the world as a whole.*

The apex of the system was to be the Bank for International Settlements in Basel, Switzerland, a private bank owned and controlled by the world's central banks, which were themselves private corporations.

Each central bank sought to dominate its government by its ability to control treasury loans, to manipulate foreign exchanges, to influence the level of economic activity in the country, and to influence co-operative politicians by subsequent rewards in the business world."

SWIFT Act proposals send a message to Wall Street and financial interests around the world.

The message is that SWIFT Act marks the beginning of the end of the tyranny of global finance.

Globalism has been revealed as an ideology of financiers, who profit from the destruction of national economies through offshoring.

Wall Street and U.S. Multinationals have made billions from offshoring and financial speculation.

This *Wall Street/Trade complex* profits from offshoring, and openly sides with China in driving the deindustrialization of America.

Like the battles at Lexington and Concord in 1776, I believe SWIFT Act will come to be known as the shot heard round the world.

SWIFT Act proposals are a road map to long term economic recovery.

Passing those proposals into law will require an epic battle with banks and financial interests that control our government through money in politics.

We need 10 to 20 million signatures on the SWIFT Act petition.

Please visit our website at swiftact.com, and consider adding your endorsement online.

Wall Street, Trade, and the New Economy

Problem

The U.S. economy has been transformed, from one based on manufacturing and high wages, to one based on low wage jobs in the service sector, easy credit, and cheap imports from low wage countries.

From independence and for more than a hundred years after the Civil War, high wages created consumer demand for American production that generated employment in manufacturing.

That system has been replaced by a New Economy in which high wage manufacturing jobs have been replaced by low wage jobs in the service sector.

In the process, the loss of wage income has been offset by
- the large scale entry of women into the workforce,
- inflows of cheap imports from low wage countries, and
- the growth of credit and long term debt

The use of debt to maintain consumer demand isn't sustainable. The limits of debt driven growth were reached in 2007, when consumer spending began to decline.

Thereafter, the inflated prices that defined the housing bubble collapsed, bringing the financial crisis of 2008 and the Great Recession that continues to the present day.

Mechanism

Financialization is the process whereby finance has overtaken industrial production as the engine of economic growth.

For example, in 1950 manufacturing profits accounted for 50 percent of U.S. domestic profits, while finance accounted for only 15 percent.

Fifty years later, these ratios had been reversed.

In 2005, financial profits accounted for 44 percent of all domestic profits, while profits from manufacturing accounted for only 11 percent.

An economy dominated by finance can't create enough jobs. Wages aren't going up and there is every sign the Great Recession is here to stay.

Causes

No. 1:
Slow Growth / Anti-inflation Policy
Federal Reserve policy has been central to shaping an economy based more on finance than production.

In the late 1970s and early 1980s, Federal Reserve Chairman Paul Volcker used extremely high interest rates to induce recession.

This policy was an attempt to use high unemployment to overcome inflation, because wages typically decline or at least stop growing during a recession.

The policy has long since been hailed as a success, but was significantly aided by the context of falling oil prices.

Between 1980 and 1986, the price of oil fell by 71 percent. In the same period, the rate of inflation fell by 70 percent.

Yet, the public was persuaded by the idea that high wages, not high oil prices, were the primary cause of runaway inflation.

Here we reach an odd juncture in the impact of ideas on our political culture.

When oil prices and other costs are stable, it is undeniable that rising wages can drive inflation.

What seems extraordinary is that an inflation crisis driven largely by oil prices was used to justify a policy of using high interest rates to limit the growth of wages.

This was the slow growth / anti-inflation policy of the Federal Reserve.

From the mid-1980s through the late 1990s, unemployment was intentionally driven to levels high enough to keep wages from growing, and keep inflation well below 4 percent.

This shift marked a fundamental change in economic policy.

Manufacturing and small business do best in an environment with moderate unemployment and mild inflation.

The reason is that wage growth that drives mild inflation also drives consumption, which is good for business.

In contrast, high unemployment brings a fall in consumption, which serves to undermine profits and acts to discourage investment.

If high unemployment and low wages are bad for business, why would the Federal Reserve work to achieve that result?

The answer is that high unemployment and low inflation serve the interests of the financial sector.

Because inflation erodes the value of money used to pay back loans, Wall Street supports anti-inflation policy as a way to guarantee financial profits.

To understand the importance of the shift in Fed policy, consider long term rates of average growth.

In the hundred years before 1970, which included the period of the Great Depression, the average annual rate of growth was 3.4 percent.

In contrast, Alan Greenspan (Federal Reserve chair 1987 – 2006) considered the non-inflationary rate of growth to be 2.5 percent.

Average economic growth of 2.5 percent is *26 percent slower* than the historic average rate of growth that prevailed when America became an industrial power.

In essence, the Fed's anti-inflation policy amounted to using high unemployment and slow growth to keep inflation at very low levels.

Since the 1970s, the U.S. economy has lost trillions of dollars in production value from this overall slower rate of economic growth.

No. 2: Shareholder Value
Since the 1980s Wall Street rules have created incentives to maximize the *short term* value of corporations.

This focus on what is called *shareholder value* places more importance on rising prices for company stock than on higher output of production.

In the 1980s corporate CEOs and top management were granted compensation in the form of stock options.

What followed was a prolonged period of downsizing and large scale layoffs.

Eliminating manufacturing divisions brought cost savings through
- reduction of the workforce, and
- reduced spending on research and development.

Each wave of downsizing resulted in higher stock prices, because stock values are based on the *present value* of company assets.

Essentially, companies that are highly liquid have higher stock values than companies that have assets tied up in long term investments.

As CEOs rushed to increase liquidity (thereby increasing the value of their stock options), downsizing became the swan song of American industry.

The trend also provided the context for offshoring, as new investments in manufacturing were shifted to low wage countries.

Thus, the decline of American industry financed the rise in stock values, as corporate restructuring was used to raise the price of company shares.

No. 3: Financial Deregulation
Financial deregulation and the absence of regulation for new forms of finance have spawned an unprecedented expansion of debt and financial speculation.

In the late 1980s Alan Greenspan established a system of creating *credit without reserves*, by changing liquidity requirements for banks.

Liquidity ratios measure how sound banks are in their ability to pay short term obligations out of cash.

In 1945, commercial banks had reserves and vault cash equivalent to 12 percent of assets, with most assets held in low risk government bonds.

This meant the banking sector as a whole had a liquidity ratio of 12 percent.

In 2007, this liquidity ratio of bank reserves to total assets was only 0.6 percent, at a time when bank assets were held in high risk derivatives and mortgage backed securities.

This change allowed the financial system to create an unprecedented volume of credit – over $50 trillion of debt in 2007.

It is hardly coincidence that trillions of lost growth in production has been offset by trillions of expanded credit in the financial sector.

This change reveals the mechanism whereby the New Economy relies on consumption based on credit and long term debt, as a substitute for consumption based on wage growth in productive industry.

Against this background of unprecedented expansion of credit, Federal Reserve and Treasury Department officials lobbied Congress to
1. overturn the Glass-Steagall Act that required separation of banks and securities dealers, and
2. prohibit the regulation of derivatives

Repeal of Glass-Steagall allowed the expanded credit available to banks to be allocated, not to more lending, but instead to speculation in highly leveraged financial investments.

In the same period, financial derivatives evolved in ways that allowed companies to report *current earnings* based on *projections of future income.*

The practice was used to overstate earnings and thereby raise the price of company shares.

No. 4: Asset Inflation Policy
This policy environment of expanded credit and financial deregulation brought unprecedented booms in stock prices.

In the mid-1990s these booms were led by speculative bubbles that emerged in the internet and telecommunications sectors.

In 2000 the dot.com bubble collapsed, bringing losses of some $5 trillion on the NASDAQ stock exchange.

Between 2000 and 2003, stocks of telecommunications companies declined by $2.8 trillion.

The response from Fed chair Alan Greenspan was to drastically cut interest rates, from 6.5 percent in 2000 down to 1 percent in 2003.

This response was *an intentional strategy* of offsetting the collapse in the dot.com and telecom sectors by creating a boom in the housing market.

In the process, Greenspan made public statements about his belief that the housing market was immune to speculation, due to the high transaction costs required for mortgages.

He also gave speeches on the virtues of adjustable rate mortgages, while refusing to crack down on predatory lending that was known to occur in refinancing.

Both Greenspan and his successor, Ben Bernanke, made public statements to the effect they anticipated interest rates to remain low for a long period.

In essence, both Greenspan and Bernanke were selling the housing boom as a cure for the collapse of the dot.com and telecom sectors.

The reality is the Federal Reserve has resorted to supporting debt financed consumption and *asset price inflation* as the basis for economic growth.

Sales of stocks and houses at inflated prices are included in annual growth statistics.

In the period leading to the 2008 crisis, fully half of reported economic growth was based on unsustainably high values in stock and house prices.

Sadly, what we call the New Economy is *structurally dependent* on financial speculation.

With expanded credit and financial deregulation, Wall Street rules provided incentives for offshoring, downsizing, mergers and acquisitions, and other forms of financial engineering.

These changes marked a new era of *financialization*, in which expanded production has been replaced by expansion of finance as the primary source of growth.

Financialization has brought fundamental restructuring of the economy, by undermining wages and slowing down the overall rate of real growth (e.g., expanded output).

In the process, the agency role of government has been transformed, because the interests represented by official policy have changed.

Government policy has abandoned the goal of industrial expansion and full employment.

Instead, official policy of both Republican and Democratic administrations, promotes debt financed consumption and asset inflation as the engine of growth.

In this way the New Economy model of growth serves the interests of the finance sector, at the expense of productive industry.

Truth and Consequences

The Federal Reserve has succeeded in transferring inflation from the price of goods and services (product inflation) to the price of assets (asset inflation).

The impact of the change has been profound.

For the generation of Americans that Tom Brokaw calls the Greatest Generation, financial security was based on

- long term employment in an economy based on manufacturing,
- earning a lifetime pension,
- paying off the mortgage on the family home, and
- paying off any other debt

For the New Economy generation, the basic ingredients of financial security look quite different.

First, short term employment in an economy based on finance is now considered normal.

Instead of a pension with guaranteed benefits, employees are given 401(k) plans that are tied to the stock market and typically pay only a fraction of pension benefits.

Depending on where you live, the difference might be offset by high real estate prices that raise the value of your home.

If you accumulate enough equity in your home, you can sell that asset over time by taking out a reverse mortgage to supplement your retirement.

But when asset prices stop rising, political crisis follows.

The reason is that the public has been sold on the idea that the financial economy, based on easy credit and rising asset prices, is a viable substitute for the real economy, based on manufacturing, high wages, and long term employment.

Impact of the New Economy

Since the 1970s:

- Slow and distorted growth has cost the economy $15 trillion in lost production.

- Wages, as a share of the economy overall, have declined by 8 percent.

- Net business investment has declined by 47 percent.

- Corporate profits have increased by 63 percent.

- The economy's capacity to create jobs, for every percentage point of overall growth, has declined by 65 percent.

This is the statistical reality of the New Economy.

The economy has been stripped of manufacturing capacity through a process of de-industrialization, marked by record trade deficits with low wage countries.

Global Connection

There is an important context in which unprecedented trade deficits have come to be ignored by policy makers.

Federal budget deficits are financed with foreign money, through the international balance of payments.

This system is based on the U.S. dollar as the international reserve currency, and is described in detail in Volume 3.

The way the system operates, U.S. trade deficits are offset by inflows of foreign capital.

It would not be possible to run budget deficits in the trillions of dollars without these inflows of foreign money.

Borrowing foreign capital to finance budget deficits makes up the system known as the Twin Deficits.

Presidents from Reagan to Obama have relied on this system of Twin Deficits to run budget deficits without raising taxes.

Equally important, the Twin Deficits system has allowed successive administrations to run budget deficits without the consequences of inflation.

Traditionally, large scale borrowing to finance budget deficits would have been inflationary, due to the increased demand for money.

Budget deficits in Reagan's first term came at a time when global markets were flooded with petro-dollars created by excess profits in the oil producing countries.

As a consequence there was no shortage of foreign inflows of capital to finance the budget deficit, so that government borrowing proved not to be inflationary.

Over time the source of foreign capital has varied, from excess profits generated by oil revenues to those generated by low wage labor and by foreign governments engaged in currency manipulation.

Regardless, successive administrations have ignored the trade deficit for the sake of political expediency.

Moreover, trade deficits are functional not only to financing government debt, but also to the logic of policy that frames the New Economy.

In fact, cheap imports are essential to the low inflation, slow growth economy that maintains financial profits at the expense of manufacturing.

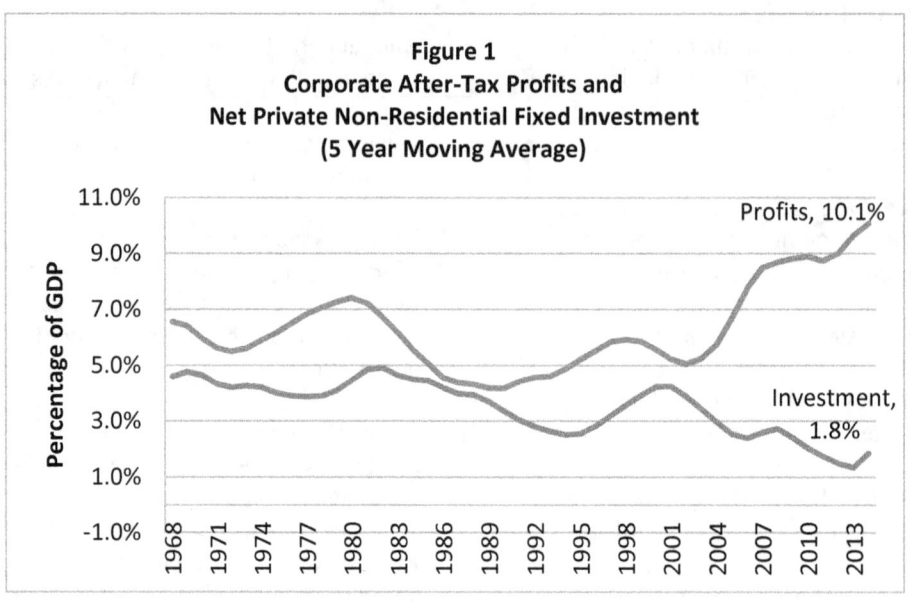

Source: Bureau of Economic Analysis.

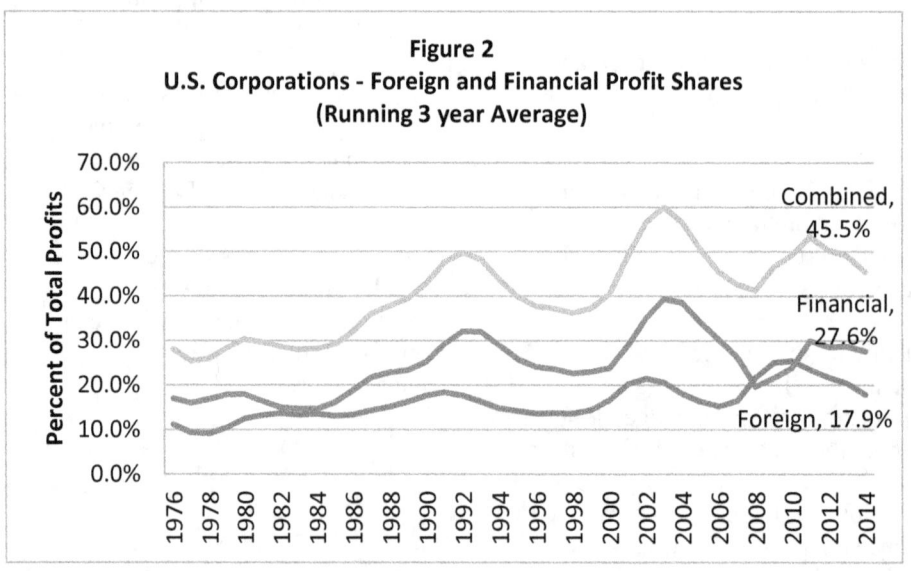

Source: Bureau of Economic Analysis: Corporate Profits by Industry
Financial profit as a percentage of total domestic profits. Foreign profits as
a percentage of total profits

The Wall Street / Trade Complex

Offshoring has brought record profits for Wall Street and U.S. companies with offshore production.

This *Wall Street / Trade complex* has made billions in profits, at the expense of American industry.

In the 1990s, removal of restrictions on capital flows created unprecedented foreign investment that drove economic booms throughout Asia.

These booms ultimately collapsed, bringing bailouts by the International Monetary Fund (IMF).

At the same time, economic reforms were imposed on debtor countries receiving IMF assistance.

For example, conditions of IMF assistance included
- high interest rates, and
- currency devaluation

High rates of interest were used to *attract foreign investment and reduce consumption*.

This restructuring created a surplus of trade for debtor countries, generating foreign exchange that was needed for loan payments.

The effect was to prevent the development of export markets for American goods.

While American manufacturing suffered the loss of markets, restructuring the economies of debtor countries was designed to guarantee repayment of loans to Western banks.

Officials at the IMF and the U.S. Treasury intentionally engineered devaluation of developing country currencies.

Currency devaluation supports the model of export led growth in the developing world, which exacerbates offshoring and undermines U.S. manufacturing.

The poor countries involved have trade surpluses, because they are prevented from developing internal markets for their own production, much less markets for imports.

In this way the status quo (trade surpluses for low wage countries, mirrored by trade deficits and industrial decline for the U.S.) is maintained.

Currency devaluation leaves this imbalance as a lasting legacy of financial sector dominance in world affairs.

The countries involved can't generate demand for American goods, because they aren't *developing* in the true sense of the word.

Figure 1 shows U.S. corporate profits are at record levels, while domestic investment is at an all-time low.

Figure 2 shows foreign and financial profits account for roughly 50 percent of corporate profits overall.

Taken together, these two figures provide a snapshot of the Wall Street / Trade complex.

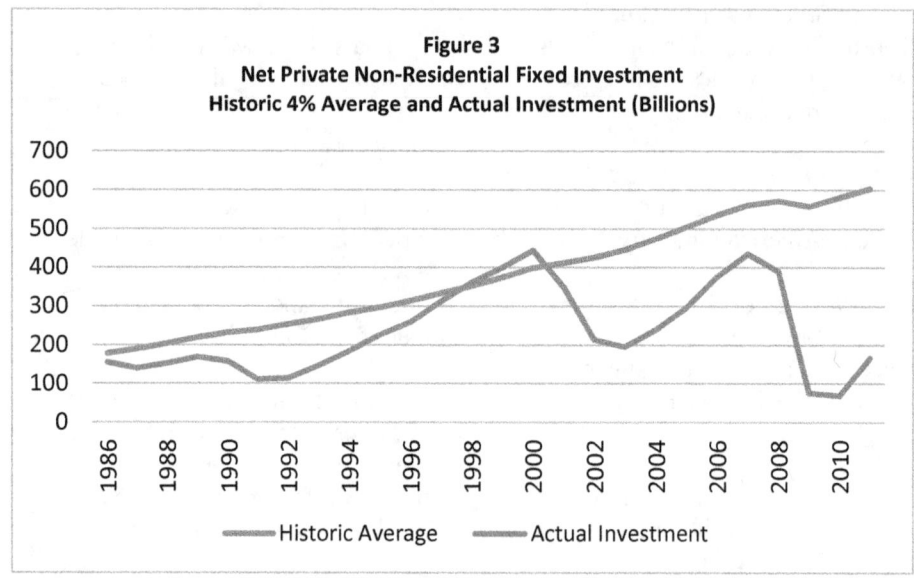

Source: Investment from Bureau of Economic Analysis; GDP from National Income and Product Accounts.

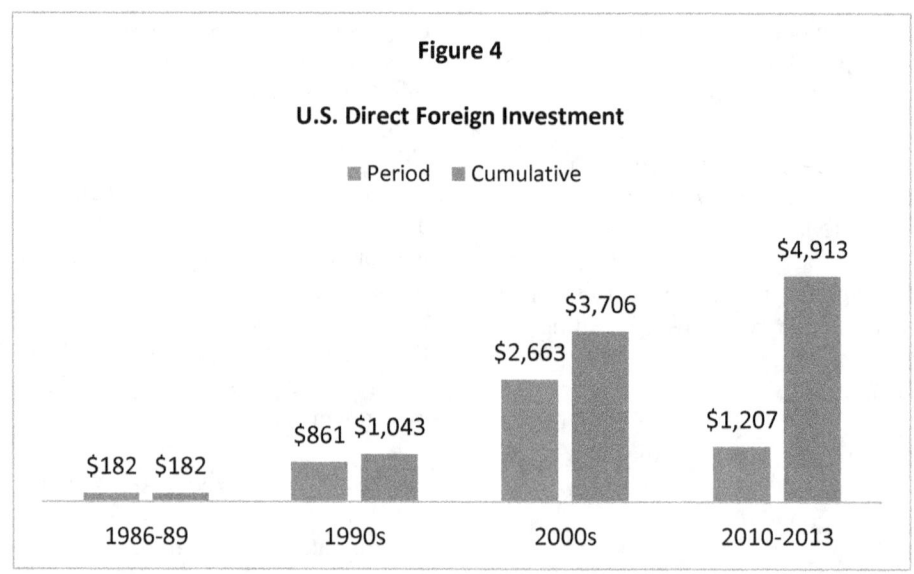

Source: Bureau of Economic Analysis

Considering financial profits, there is clear evidence that corporations have increasingly used profits to buy stocks instead of making productive investments.

For example, between 1970 and 1979 non-financial firms spent $1.30 on stock investments for every $1 dollar spent on productive investment.

Twenty years later, the ratio had changed dramatically.

Between 1998 and 2007, non-financial firms spent $27 on stock trading for every $1 dollar allocated to productive investment.

At the same time, about a quarter of the amount spent on financial investments was borrowed.

These non-financial firms were not only shifting away from productive investment, but were also taking on debt to leverage investments in finance.

Speculative finance has had a corrupting influence, even for non-financial business.

The end result has been a diversion of domestic investment away from productive industry.

The corresponding trend has been the rise in productive investment overseas, as companies shifted production to countries with low wages and minimal regulation of industry.

Between 1960 and 1984, net non-residential fixed investment averaged 4 percent per year.

Figure 3 shows the difference between the historic average and actual investment, called the investment gap.

The *cumulative* loss of domestic investment represented by that gap comes to over $4 trillion dollars since the mid-1980s.

In 2013 net private non-residential fixed investment was less than 2 percent of GDP, with an investment gap over $338 billion dollars.

At the same time, while domestic investment has declined, U.S. foreign investment has been rising.

Figure 4 shows U.S. direct foreign investment.

In 2013 the investment gap for the U.S. economy was $338 billion, while U.S. foreign investment was $311 billion.

Since the mid-1980s, the *cumulative* loss of investment for the U.S. economy was $4 trillion, while the *cumulative* total for foreign investment was $4.9 trillion.

Not surprisingly, there is a very close match between the two sets of figures.

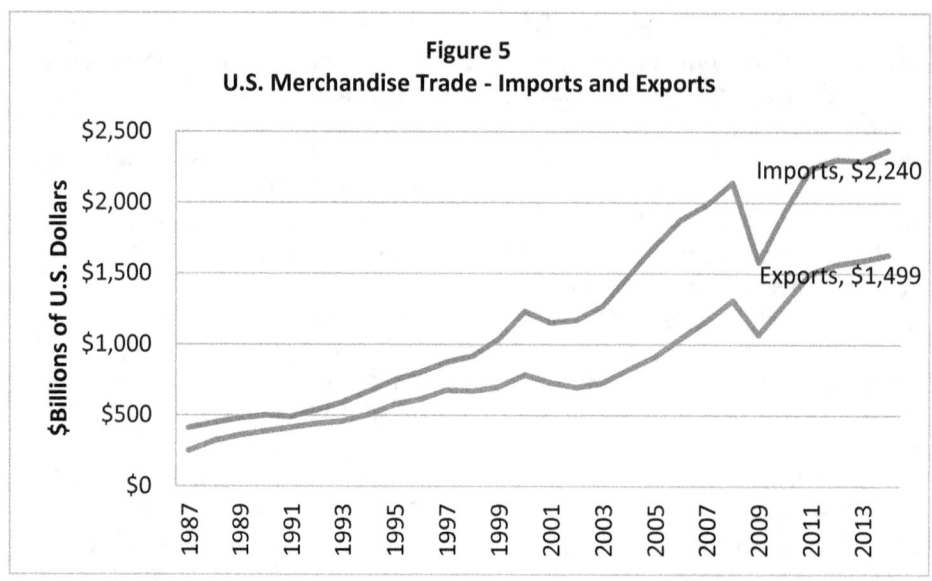

Figure 5
U.S. Merchandise Trade - Imports and Exports

U.S. Census Bureau

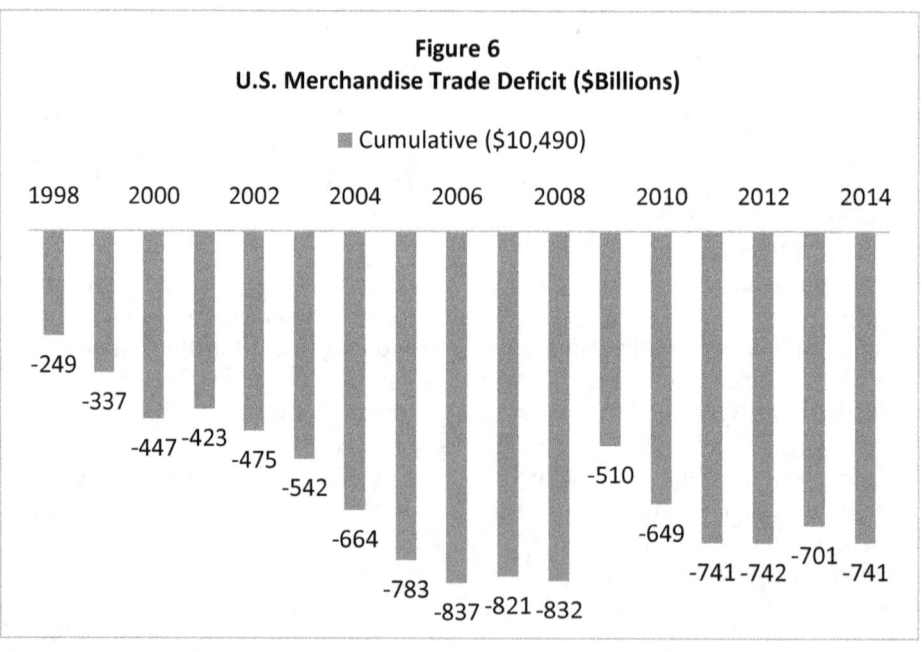

Figure 6
U.S. Merchandise Trade Deficit ($Billions)

Source: U.S. Census Bureau

As offshoring has moved manufacturing overseas, investment has been shifted outside the country.

The Wall Street / Trade complex has financial interest in a system that undermines American industry.

America's national interest is not served by allowing unlimited campaign contributions from corporations that profit from offshoring and financial speculation.

Bipartisan Consensus
The most important sign of American decline is the trade deficit.

Figure 5 shows the value of merchandise imports and exports.

We have a trade deficit because we import more than we export.

Because offshoring has undermined U.S. productive capacity, expanded trade means imports will always grow faster than exports.

Trying to create jobs through exports is like picking up a bucket that has holes in the bottom and trying to fill it up with water.

Yet, candidates in both parties proclaim that trade creates jobs.

The reality is that *exports* create jobs. When imports are greater than exports, the net result is job loss.

For the question below, there is only one correct answer.

Which of the following is true?
a) Trade creates jobs.
b) Exports create jobs.

The correct answer is b) Exports create jobs.

The correct answer is a verifiable fact, and isn't something that depends on how liberal or conservative the person answering might be.

The statement "Trade creates jobs" isn't true when Republicans say it, and it isn't true when Democrats say it either.

Along the same lines, politicians in both parties can be quoted as saying they think "on balance, trade creates jobs."

"On balance" is certainly the key to solving the riddle.

On balance, in 2014 we imported over $741 billion more than we exported in goods.

That's called a $741 billion dollar trade deficit in goods.

Figure 6 shows the cumulative deficit in the goods trade, (also called merchandise trade), since 1998 is over $10 trillion dollars.

That isn't the total amount imported, but just the amount over and above the value of goods we exported to the rest of the world.

Every dollar spent on imports is a dollar that can't be spent domestically to support American jobs.

"On balance," politicians from both parties think sending $10 trillion over seas, instead of spending it domestically to create jobs in this country, is a good thing.

Politics of Status Quo
There has been no meaningful reform of the Wall Street rules that create incentives for offshoring to low wage countries.

Corporate CEOs are granted hundreds of millions of dollars in stock options, as the doctrine of shareholder value still prevails.

The Volcker rule, which requires separation between banks and securities dealers, was severely weakened in the final form of the Dodd Frank financial reform.

The top banks are larger today than before the 2008 crisis, and pose as much risk to the economy today as they did before the crisis.

Like the Volcker rule pertaining to banks, regulation of derivatives trading was also limited in the Dodd Frank reform bill.

Then in 2015 the Obama administration passed a budget deal that backs derivatives trading with federal deposit insurance.

The result is the very banks that remain too big to fail, continue to profit from high risk bets on derivatives, while lending for domestic investment remains stagnant.

Wall Street and U.S. Multinationals have made billions in profit from downsizing, layoffs, and offshoring.

The decline of American industry has been made profitable through the enactment of Wall Street rules.

Those rules grant stock options to CEOs, make borrowed money used for corporate takeovers tax deductible, and allow unrestricted trade in derivatives.

Both political parties, both houses of Congress, the Federal Reserve, the Treasury Department, and the executive branch all serve financial sector interests on Wall Street.

Politics of Reform
The problem with our economy has nothing to do with the differences between liberals and conservatives.

What we need is a presidential contest in which candidates from both parties oppose unrestricted trade and unlimited subsidies for Wall Street banks.

If you are a committed Democrat or Republican, you might consider working within your party to nominate reform candidates who share those views.

The cost of the Wall Street bail out, begun under George W. Bush and continued under Barack Obama, amounted to over $7.8 trillion dollars.

The reality is we already have industrial policy, in the form of too big to fail and the ongoing efforts of the Federal Reserve to prop up real estate values in the housing market.

Acknowledging that reality means admitting there is nothing fundamentally liberal or conservative about such policy.

What we see is bipartisan support for what amounts to a globalist ideology that promotes offshoring and the ceding of sovereignty to global financial interests.

The problems we face can be solved, by restructuring the economy through investments in manufacturing and through taxes on imports and Wall Street financial transactions.

America can return to a position of pre-eminence and leadership around the world, instead of courting bankruptcy and ceding national autonomy to the sovereign bond market.

If you prefer the former to the later, you might consider giving your support to SWIFT Act legislation.

SWIFT Act Development Initiative (SWIFT Act)

SWIFT Act proposals are revenue neutral, and are based on 5 core principles.

Smart Growth

Permanent recovery can only be achieved through revival of the real economy, led by manufacturing and high technology, high-value-added industries.

Recovery will also require reducing the trade deficit and reforming the financial sector to fundamentally restructure the national economy.

Wage Standards

Imposing wage standards on imports will prohibit unfair wage competition and reduce offshoring.

Wage standards will also raise foreign demand for American goods by requiring higher wages in the export sectors of our trading partners.

Industrial Policy

Strategic promotion of manufacturing and advanced technology industry is critical to U.S. competitiveness in world markets.

National security includes not only military security, but economic security as well.

Federal government responsibility for the national welfare is a mandate for supporting key industries that can serve as the basis for future prosperity.

Strategic development should be established as a national priority through creation of a cabinet Department of Economic Development.

Financial Reform

Unprecedented growth of the financial sector has reduced incentive for productive investment and diminished the economy's capacity to create jobs.

At the same time, Wall Street interests and too-big-to-fail banks have successfully lobbied to block meaningful reform.

First, size limitations should be imposed to break up the banks, reduce systemic risk, and prevent future bailouts.

Second, the financial sector should be subject to taxes designed to establish parity between returns from financial investment and needed investments in productive industry.

Third, compensating corporate executives with stock options should be outlawed.

Fourth, the Consumer Financial Protection Bureau should establish a voluntary pension plan for private sector employees.

Fifth, the Citizens United ruling that allows unlimited contributions to political campaigns should be repealed.

Trade and Tax Reform

A U.S. VAT would tax imports and but not exports in the same way the VAT is used in over 150 countries around the world.

The effect would create incentive for investment in manufacturing, and disincentive for offshoring.

Companies would have more incentive to conduct manufacturing in this country, and less incentive to import from abroad.

Smart Growth

Main Points

In 2015, the economy grew at an annual rate of just two percent.

Two percent growth is only 60 percent of the historic average rate of 3.4 percent established between 1870 and 1973.

Over time, slow and distorted growth has cost the economy more than $15 trillion dollars in productive value.

Since the 1970s, there has also been progressive decline in the economy's capacity to create jobs.

The jobs/GDP ratio is a measure of the relationship between GDP growth and job growth.

While both wages and the jobs/GDP ratio peaked in the 1970s, since then both have shown progressive decline.

From 2011 through 2014, the jobs/GDP ratio re-bounded, to a little more than 2.8 percent.

That recovery puts the ratio back on par with where it was in the period between 2000 and 2007, but still only a little more than a third of the jobs/GDP ratio in the 1970s.

Compared to the 1970s, the economy's capacity to create jobs has declined by 65 percent.

The economy's declining capacity to create jobs is a direct result of the decline in manufacturing.

Between 1998 and 2010, direct employment in manufacturing declined by six million jobs.

Direct job loss in manufacturing brought additional loss of 10 million jobs in supply chains, and loss of another 7 million jobs from lack of re-spending throughout the economy.

The combined impact was the loss of more than 23 million jobs.

Offshoring and the loss of manufacturing have brought a loss of productive capacity.

The economy's capacity to create wealth and jobs has declined, because investments that should have been made in productive industry have been used instead for speculative finance or foreign investment.

Without slow and distorted growth, there would be no budget deficits.

Smart growth reflects acknowledgement that slow and distorted growth is the problem, and that permanent recovery will require economic restructuring.

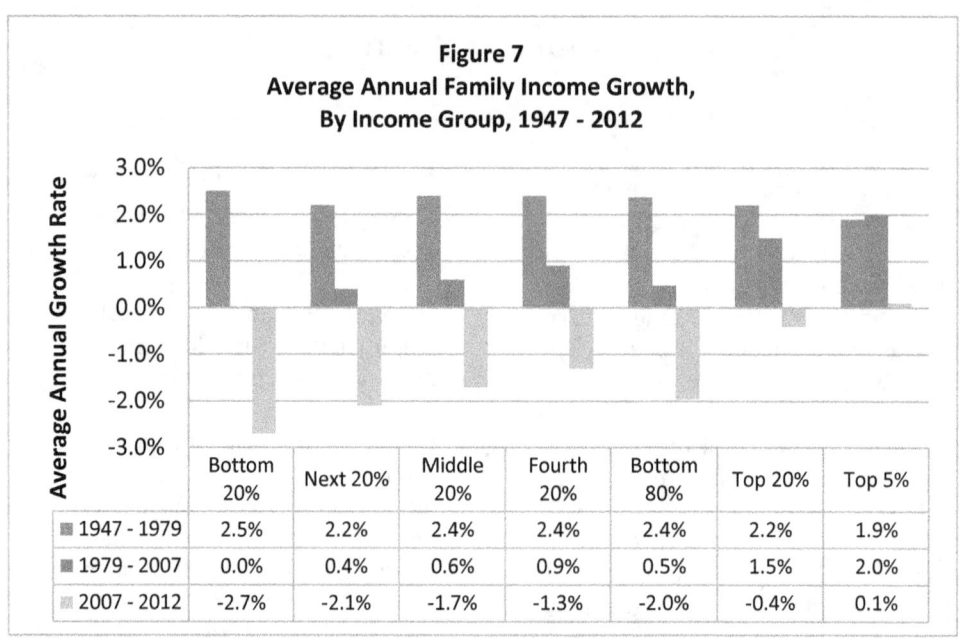

Source: Elise Gould (2014). Why America's Workers Need Faster Wage Growth--
And What We Can Do About It. (Washington, D.C.: Economic Policy Institute),
Briefing Paper #382, page 9.

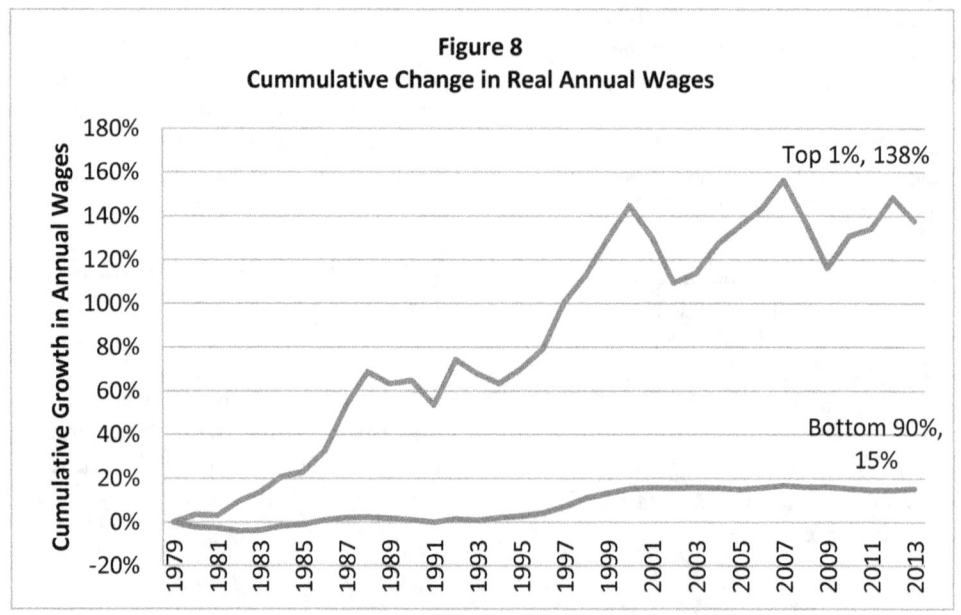

Source: Lawrence Mishel, Elise Gould, and Josh Bivens (2015). Charting Wage
Stagnation in Nine Charts. (Washington, D.C.: Economic Policy Institute).
EPI analysis of data from Kopczuk, Saez, and Song (2010) and Social Security
Administration wage statistics. Reproduced from Figure F in Raising America's
Pay: Why It's Our Central Economic Policy Challenge.

Since the mid-1990s, economic growth has been based on rising stock and house prices.

This asset price inflation has increased the value of financial wealth, but done little to grow the economy in terms of productive value.

Corporate profits today are more than 60 percent higher than the average rate of the 1950s.

While corporate profits have risen to record levels, income and wages have declined.

Figure 7 shows annual *family income growth* from 1947 through 2012, broken down by family income group.

Between 1947 and 1979, for the bottom 80 percent of families, average annual income growth was 2.375 percent.

In the period between 1979 and 2007, for the bottom 80 percent of families, average annual income growth was 0.475 percent (less than half of one percent).

That change in the rate of income growth represents a decline of 80 percent.

Note that in the period between 1947 and 1979, the economy was based on manufacturing.

But in the period between 1979 and 2007, the economy was gutted by the loss of manufacturing through offshoring.

Over nearly 30 years, annual income growth, for the bottom 80 percent of families, grew at a rate that was 80 percent slower than the average rate in the 30 years prior to 1979.

This dramatic change took place before the Wall Street financial crisis of 2008.

Figure 8 shows annual income growth *by wage group.*

*Between 1979 and 2006, income growth for the top one tenth of one percent (0.01%) was **20 times faster** than that of the bottom 90% of wage earners.*

If income growth had continued unchanged from the average rate for 1947 – 1979, median household income in 2007 would have been higher by nearly $18,000 dollars.

Yet even this magnitude of difference for *household* income ignores the fact that women only began entering the workforce in large numbers in the 1970s.

The fact is, prior to the 1970s household income was based on one income.

In 2007 median household income was nearly $18,000 lower than it would have been if the growth rates of 1947-1979 had continued, despite the prevalence today of two income households.

Source: Federal Reserve Bank of St. Louis.

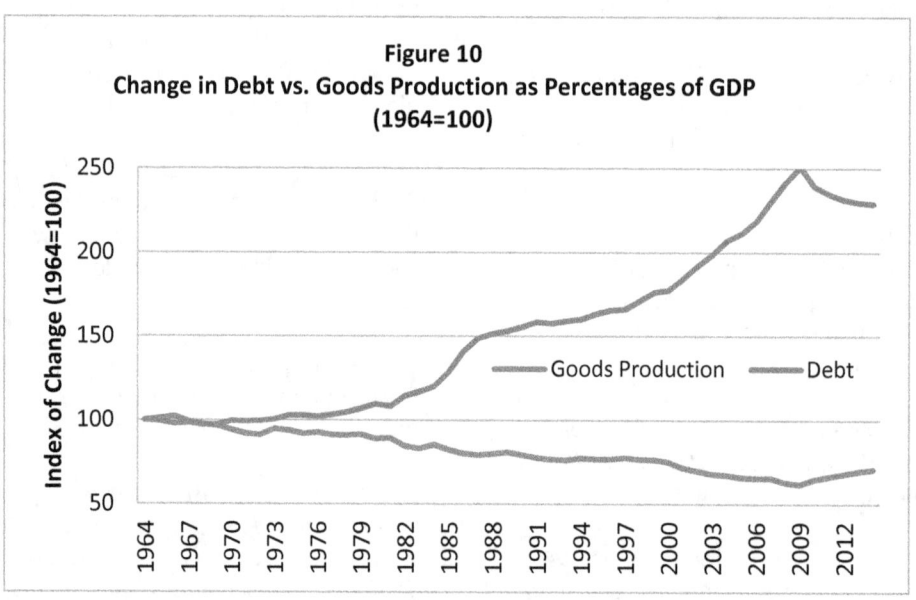

Sources: Calculated from Federal Reserve, Flow of Funds Accounts of the United States, "Credit Market Debt Outstanding," Table L.1; Economic Report of the President, 2013, "Gross Domestic Product by Major Type of Product, 1964-2012," Table B.8; Economic Report of the President, 2015, "Gross Domestic Product, 2000-2014," Table B.2; and U.S. Bureau of Economic Analysis, "Real Gross Domestic Product: Goods: Percent Change."

Inequality is also more than simply an issue of fairness.

Low income families spend by far the largest proportion of their incomes on consumption.

So while the economy depends on consumption, the pattern of growth for more than 30 years has resulted in a decreasing share of income for those who spend the most on consumption.

Figure 9 shows the proportion of wages and salaries in the economy, referred to as the wage share of GDP.

In the 28 years between 1947 and 1974, annual wages and salaries averaged 51.5 percent of GDP.

The wage share of GDP fell below 50 percent in 1974 and has been declining ever since, averaging 43 percent since 2009.

The difference between the historic average and the recent average rate is 8 percent of GDP.

In 2014, 8 percent of GDP amounted to more than $1.3 trillion dollars.

Today *annual* wages from employment are $1.3 trillion less than they would be if the proportion of wage income in the economy was at 1973 levels.

In the New Economy, growth is no longer defined in terms of rising output and employment, with demand supported by actual purchasing power.

As shown in Figure 10, the decline in goods production has been accompanied by rising debt.

Fully half of the New Economy is artificial, in which growth is fueled by debt and speculation.

Displacement of productive enterprise by speculation and financial engineering, along with the erosion of our tax base that results, is the hallmark of the New Economy.

Yet, political debate centers on the budget deficit, instead of reversing decades of distorted growth that created it.

Slow and Distorted Growth
Clearly, growth statistics that include expansion based on rising asset prices overstate the actual growth in the underlying economy.

Since the 1970s, there has been a decline in the overall rate of GDP growth, coupled with changes that reflect much more rapid growth of the financial sector.

Between 1870 and 1973, the U.S. economy grew at an average annual rate, including the period of the Great Depression, of 3.4 percent.

That was the inflation adjusted average rate of growth from the period after the civil war, spanning more than a century of our economic development.

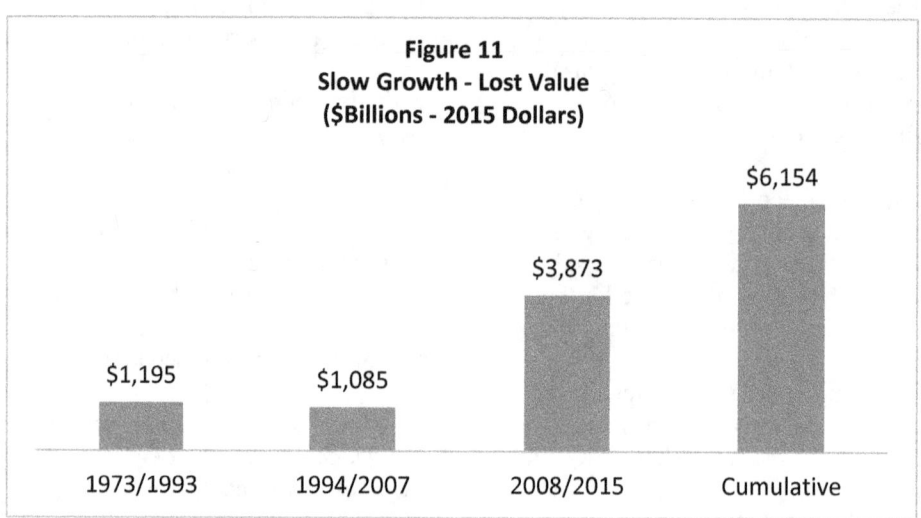

Figure 11
Slow Growth - Lost Value
($Billions - 2015 Dollars)

Source: Economic Research Service, USDA (2012). Real Historical Gross Domestic Product (GDP) and Growth Rates of GDP for Basline Countries/Regions. Based on World Bank World Development Indicators, International Financial Statistics of the IMF, IHS Global Insight, and Oxford Economic Forecasting, as well as estimated values developed by the Economic Research Service. Author's calculation of difference between 3.4% historic average rate of growth and growth rates cited.

Between 1973 and 1993, the average rate of growth fell to 2.9 percent.

That decline of 0.6 percent means the economy was growing at a rate *nearly 13 percent slower* than the historic average rate of growth.

Then between 1993 and 2016, the average rate of growth fell to a little less than 2.5 percent.

Over the past 20 years, the economy has been growing 26 percent more slowly than the historic average.

Finally, in the four years between 2012 and 2016, the average rate of growth fell to just 2 percent.

Two percent annual growth is more than 40 percent slower than the historic average.

Official statements aside, the economy can't generate enough jobs at the current rate of growth.

In 2015, eight years after the onset of recession, the economy grew at an annual rate of only 2 percent.

My estimates rely on official figures, which may well understate the economic damage caused by slower growth overall.

Using the government's own data, Figure 11 shows the economic damage done by slow growth since 1973.

As of year-end 2015, slow growth has created a cumulative loss of more than $6.1 trillion in production value.

While decline in the rate of overall growth has been costly, the composition of growth has also been distorted by rapid growth of the financial sector.

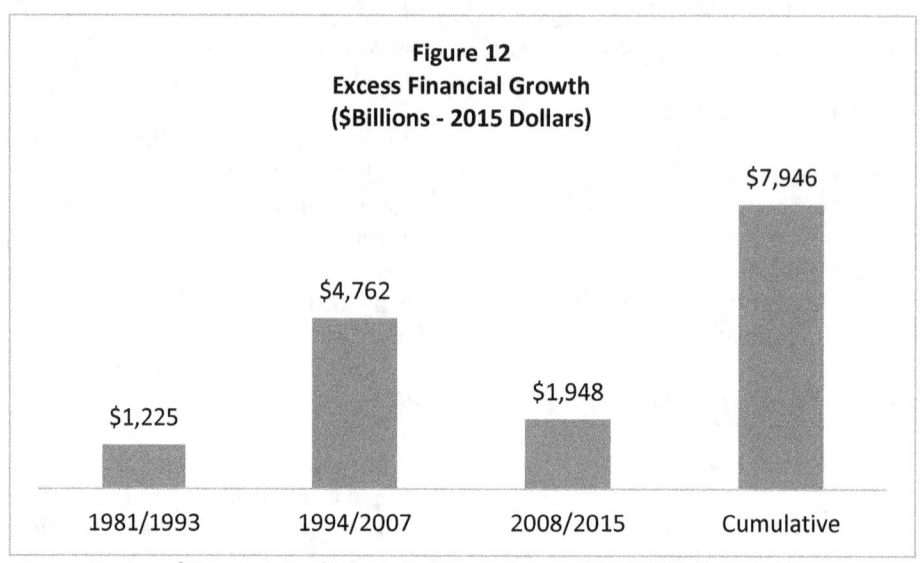

Figure 12
Excess Financial Growth
($Billions - 2015 Dollars)

Source: Bureau of Economic Analysis. Author's calculation using 1980 baseline of 4.9% value added in GDP by Financial sector.

Harvard Business School professors David Scharfstein and Robin Greenwood have tracked the rate of financial sector growth over more than 60 years.

The financial industry accounted for 2.8 percent of value added in GDP in 1950, and rose to 4.9 percent in 1980.

Since 1980, the average growth rate for the financial sector was almost double the rate in the thirty years before.

Scharfstein and Greenwood argue there is no reason the financial sector should have become less efficient in today's economy, as measured by the rising cost to other economic sectors.

Figure 12 shows the value of excess growth in the financial sector.

By 2015, excess financial sector growth, over and above the 1980 baseline, had reached a cumulative value of nearly $8 trillion dollars.

Excess financial growth of $8 trillion means that same value was not accounted for by industrial growth.

This change in the composition of growth is a measure of the New Economy, marked by consumer debt and the decline of manufacturing.

Although minor by comparison, another source of excess financial profit has been oil speculation.

After rising substantially in 2004, oil prices continued rising through 2013.

In 2011, ExxonMobil CEO Rex Tillerson testified before Congress that 40 percent of the oil price was accounted for by speculation.

The New York Times reported one estimate that speculation cost the U.S. economy $200 billion dollars a year.

The source of speculation has been special exemptions granted by the Federal Reserve, and relaxed regulations approved by Congress, that allow Wall Street banks to own non-financial businesses.

The banks now own infrastructure that includes pipelines, refineries, and fleets of oil tankers, as well as companies that control operations at major ports.

In addition to speculation in oil prices, the New York Times also reported on the role Wall Street has played in driving up the price of aluminum and other commodities.

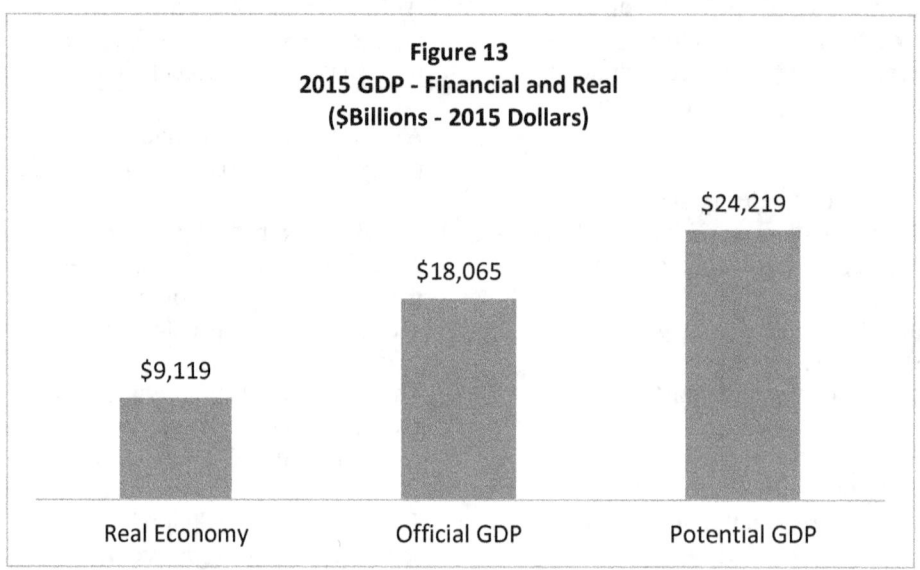

Figure 13
2015 GDP - Financial and Real
($Billions - 2015 Dollars)

Source: Author's calculation based on excess profits, and lost production value
from slow growth.

($Billions - 2015 Dollars)		
Real Economy	$9,119	
		$1,000 Oil Speculation
		$7,946 Excess Financial Growth
Excess Profits	$8,946	
Official GDP	$18,065	
Slow Growth - Lost Value	$6,154	
Potential GDP	$24,219	

Source: Author's calculation based on figures 11 and 12, and estimate of
cost of oil speculation between 2004 and 2013.

Real Economy as Percent of Official GDP: 50%

Real Economy as Percent of Potential GDP: 38%

Figure 13 shows a value estimate of the real economy, compared to official GDP.

Excess financial growth accounts for $7.9 trillion of GDP growth reported since 1973.

Without hard data on the cost of oil speculation, I used a conservative figure of $1 trillion dollars for the period between 2004 and 2013.

These figures combined total more than $8.9 trillion in excess profits.

Officially reported GDP, minus the value of excess profits, equals the value of the real economy.

Note that the real economy estimate is only 50 percent of the GDP value reported in official statistics.

This assessment shows how the real economy only makes up half of the New Economy.

The composition of growth has changed, such that excess financial growth has transformed the economy.

Combined Impact
If the economy had grown at the historic average rate established in the hundred years after the civil war, the value of GDP in 2015 would have been higher by $6.1 trillion dollars.

Adding that $6.1 trillion to the officially reported GDP generates potential GDP, which is the GDP the economy would have reached, if the historic average rate of growth had been maintained.

The difference between potential GDP and the real economy is more than $15 trillion dollars.

Slow and distorted growth has transformed society, and left us with a $15 trillion dollar hole in the economy.

The economy today is growing at less than 60 percent of the historic average rate of growth that prevailed from the 1870s to the 1970s.

Without large scale investment, there is no chance the historic 3.4 percent rate of growth, which defined America as an industrial power, can be restored.

Yet, there isn't enough demand in the economy to justify private sector investment.

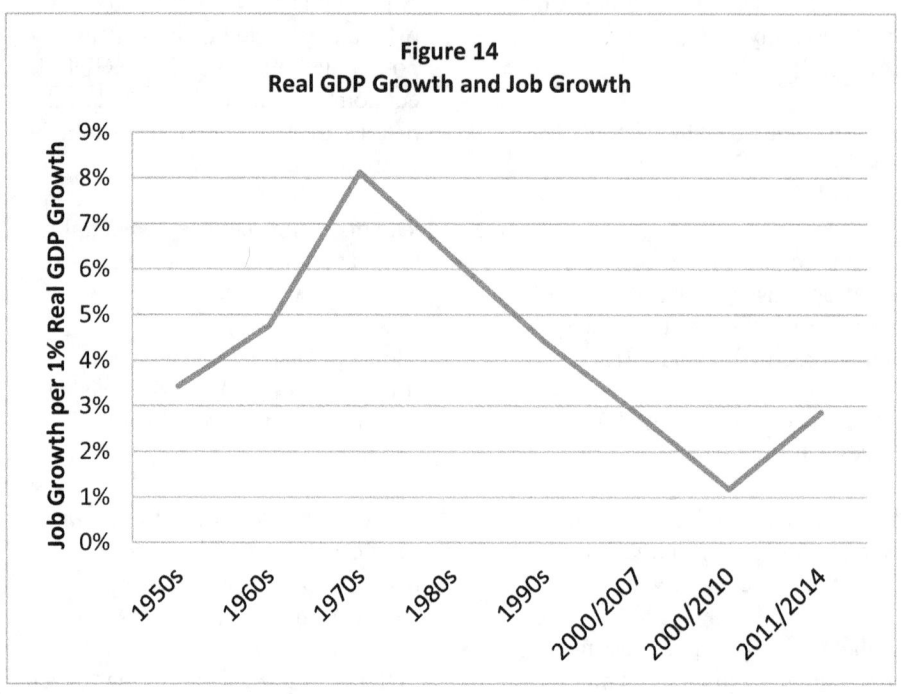

Figure 14
Real GDP Growth and Job Growth

Source: Based on Laura D'Andrea Tyson, "Jobs Deficit, Investment Deficit, Fiscal Deficit," New York Times, Economix, July 29, 2011. The percentage increase in employment reflects the net employment change as a share of total employment in the base year (e.g., 1980 for the 1980s). Updated figures for 2000s and 2011 - 2014 based on data from Bureau of Economic Analysis and Bureau of Labor Statistics.

GDP Growth and Jobs

In terms of jobs, the picture has become increasingly bleak.

Figure 14 shows job growth and GDP growth since the 1950s.

While historically employment growth has driven growth in GDP, the relationship began to change in the 1980s.

In the 1980s every percentage point of GDP growth was matched by a corresponding 6.25 percent growth in employment, a decline of nearly 25 percent compared to the 1970s.

In the 1990s employment grew by 4.4 percent for every percentage gain in GDP, only a little more than half the rate of the 1970s.

From 2000 to 2007 the ratio fell to 2.8 percent, which was a little more than a third of the jobs/GDP ratio in the 1970s.

For the period 2000-2010 the ratio was just 1.2 percent, or roughly 15 percent of the jobs/GDP ratio shown for the 1970s.

This disparity appears consistent with the growing disconnect between increasing financial wealth and growth in the underlying economy.

By the 2000s the financial sector was the driving force of stagnation in the underlying economy.

From 2011 through 2014, the jobs/GDP ratio re-bounded, to a little more than 2.8 percent.

That recovery puts the ratio back on par with where it was in the period between 2000 and 2007, but still only a little more than a third of the jobs/GDP ratio in the 1970s.

Compared to the 1970s, the economy's capacity to create jobs has declined by 65 percent.

The economy's declining capacity to create jobs is a direct result of the decline in manufacturing.

Between 1998 and 2010 over 6 million jobs were lost in manufacturing.

Four fifths of the total followed China's 2001 entry into the World Trade Organization.

The decline is especially troubling because those jobs have been lost in the most productive sector of the economy.

Figure 15
Impact of Manufacturing Job Loss
1998 - 2010 (millions of jobs)

Direct Manufacturing Jobs Lost	Supply Chain Employment	Re-spending Employment
6.0	10.0	7.0

Direct Job Loss:	6.0
Supply Chain Job Loss:	10.0
Re-spending Job Loss:	7.0
Total Loss of Employment:	23.0

Source: Josh Bivens, 2003. Updated Employment Multipliers for the U.S. Economy. (Washington, D.C.: Economic Policy Institute). No. 268, Table 8.

Figure 16
Alternative Measures of Unemployment

		July 2012 *Percent	Jul-12 Unemployed (Millions)	July 2015 *Percent	Jul-15 Unemployed (Millions)
U-1	Persons unemployed 15 weeks or longer, as a percentage of the civilian labor force	4.3%	6.7	2.0%	3.1
U-2	Job losers and persons who completed temporary jobs, as a percentage of the civilian labor force	4.6%	7.1	2.7%	4.2
U-3	Total unemployed, as a percentage of the civilian labor force (official unemployment rate)	8.6%	13.3	5.6%	8.8
U-4	U-3 plus discouraged workers, as a percentage of the civilian labor force plus discouraged workers	9.1%	14.1	6.0%	9.4
U-5	U-4 plus all other marginally attached workers, as a % of the civilian labor force plus all marginally attached	10.0%	15.5	6.7%	10.5
U-6	U-5 plus total employed part-time because full time jobs are not available	15.1%	23.4	10.8%	17.0

Source: Bureau of Labor Statistics. Persons marginally attached to the labor force are those who currently are neither working nor looking for work but indicate that they want and are available for a job and have looked for work in the past 12 months. Discouraged workers, a subset of the marginally attached, have given a job-market related reason for not currently looking for work. Persons employed part time for economic reasons are those who want and are available for full-time work but have had to settle for a part-time schedule. Figures reflect un-adjusted rates.

Figure 15 shows the cumulative loss of manufacturing jobs between 1998 and 2010.

Due to extensive product supply and distribution channels, secondary jobs are also created in support of manufacturing, called supply chain jobs.

When employees spend their paychecks, that spending also has ripple effects that support even more jobs in other areas of the economy.

Those indirect employment effects add up to a loss of more than 17 million jobs, above and beyond the loss of 6 million jobs reflecting direct employment in manufacturing.

The combined total impact comes to a loss of more than 23 million jobs between 1998 and 2010.

While it's easy enough to say the loss of manufacturing employment has been offset by job gains in other sectors, recent levels of unemployment don't support that argument.

Figure 16 shows alternative measures of unemployment.

There has been extensive criticism of the official U-3 rate as generating dramatic under-reporting of the actual level of unemployment.

For example, the official unemployment rate doesn't count marginally attached workers (temporary and short term employees) or those who only have part-time jobs.

Adding marginally attached workers and those forced to take part-time jobs to the official U-3 rate renders the U-6 rate, which in July 2012 was 15.1 percent – more than 23 million people unemployed.

U-6 data showing 23 million people unemployed was cited by Republican candidate Mitt Romney in the run up to the 2012 election.

By July 2015, the U-6 figure was reported at only 17 million unemployed, equivalent to 10.8 percent of the labor force.

Even so, a 2015 Gallup survey showed 16 percent of respondents did not have enough money to feed themselves or their family.

The conclusion is that not only are there not enough jobs, but many of the jobs being counted in the statistics don't pay enough for people to feed themselves or their families.

The number of people on food stamps reached an all-time high in 2013, and was still more than 45 million people in 2015.

By July 2016 the U-6 figure was reported at only 16 million. Even so, in 2016 there were 900,000 more people 65 and older who had jobs than there were in 2008.

When elderly people can't afford to retire and take part time jobs, they get counted in the statistics and make the official figures on unemployment lower.

The reality is the economy has been gutted by offshoring, and can no longer create enough jobs.

That means not enough jobs created, but also not enough jobs that pay well enough for people to feed themselves and their families, and not enough jobs that can fund retirement for people 65 and older.

This country's manufacturing base has been sent overseas, and the employment generated by that production has been lost.

In 2013 there were 5 million fewer jobs in manufacturing than in 1997, while in the same period manufacturing output declined by 35 percent.

Yet in 2014 the trade deficit in goods was over $741 billion dollars.

The trade deficit and job loss in manufacturing are two sides of the same coin.

Between 1998 and 2010 this country imported $7.3 trillion more in goods than it exported, with corresponding loss of 6 million jobs in manufacturing.

This extraordinary transformation has been matched by a corresponding rise of U.S. corporate profits outside this country and a corresponding fall in productive investment in the domestic economy.

Since the 1980s slow and distorted growth has generated trillions of fewer dollars in production than would have been realized at the historic average rate of growth.

Today *annual* wages from employment are $1.3 trillion less than they would be if the proportion of wage income in the economy was at pre-1974 levels.

Now without question the economy lacks the level of demand required to justify the investment we need to get things going again.

Yet corporations have some $2 trillion dollars in cash that isn't being invested.

Those productive investments aren't made when there isn't enough demand in the economy.

In the aftermath of the financial crisis, more than $7.8 trillion was provided by the Federal Reserve to prevent the collapse of the banking system.

In 2013 the Fed purchased toxic assets from Wall Street banks at the rate of $75 billion per month.

Then in 2014 Fed continued to buy toxic assets at the rate of $30 billion a month.

Yet even today the banks continue to hoard cash, and corporations are still not making the productive investments essential to job growth and economic recovery.

Wage Standards

Main Points

Wage standards should be used as one element of a multi-part strategy to reduce the leakage of demand and investment caused by offshoring.

Offshoring and foreign investment by U.S. multinationals have been driven by a wide range of incentives, including subsidies, tax advantages, undervalued foreign currencies, and low wage labor.

American industry can't compete with cheap imports, often made with wages between 50 cents and $1 an hour, and to some extent with child labor.

Even so, higher wages in the export sectors of poor countries would have limited impact on prices in the American market.

Corporations can't raise prices without losing sales, because consumers no longer have the income or even the credit to pay higher prices.

Instead, higher wages overseas would raise global demand for U.S. exports.

Increasing U.S. exports would reduce unemployment and spur growth in this country.

The result would be higher demand, in both the U.S. and abroad, which would increase sales and drive economic growth around the world.

The low wage / low demand pattern of under-development is a critical issue that impacts employment in this country.

Consumer markets that might have evolved in poor countries over the last 40 years remain under-developed.

While low wages attract U.S. multinationals, those companies make investments in the export sectors of the host countries involved.

Without labor unions or child labor laws, poor country economies reflect too little demand to support markets for American goods.

Figure 17
Household Consumption and Goods Trade Deficit by Country

Household Consumption In 2014 U.S. Dollars	Household Consumption (per capita) 2013		Trade in Goods U.S. Balance ($Billions)
Country	Per Year	Per Month	2014
Bangladesh	$497	$41	-$4,190
Chad	$515 *2005	$43	-$2,265
Pakistan	$697	$58	-$2,157
Cambodia	$714	$59	-$2,516
Vietnam	$810	$68	-$24,859
India	$842	$70	-$23,601
Bolivia	$1,017	$85	-$935
Sri Lanka	$1,277 *2010	$106	-$2,320
Indonesia	$1,278	$107	-$11,031
Philippines	$1,333	$111	-$1,699
Angola	$1,426 *2012	$119	-$3,679
Nicaragua	$1,456	$121	-$2,090
China	$1,560	$130	-$342,633
Thailand	$2,182	$182	-$15,330
Ecuador	$2,937	$245	-$2,476
Venezuela, RB	$4,254	$355	-$18,880
Malaysia	$4,345	$362	-$17,311
South Africa	$4,688 *2012	$391	-$1,921
Russian Federation	$5,406	$450	-$12,924
Saudi Arabia	$6,295	$525	-$28,359
Hungary	$6,702	$558	-$3,418
Mexico	$7,021	$585	-$53,831
Poland	$7,810	$651	-$1,519
Czech Republic	$8,185	$682	-$2,035
Trin & Tobago	$8,795 *2008	$733	-$3,578

U.S. goods deficit with countries shown: **-$585,557**

U. S. goods deficit with all countries: **-$741,462**

Percentage of goods deficit accounted for by countries shown: **79%**

Source: Household consumption from World Bank; 2013 figures for all countries except Chad (2005), Sri Lanka (2010), Angola (2012), South Africa (2012), and Trinidad & Tobago (2008). Goods trade deficit from U. S. Department of Commerce.

Figure 17 shows 25 countries with which the U.S. had a trade deficit in 2014. Private consumption *per household* is also shown.

In 2014, roughly 85 percent of the U.S. trade deficit was with countries that lack consumer markets for American goods.

There is clearly something wrong with this picture.

*In the world economy there is a **Big Lie** that low wage / low demand economies are undergoing a process of transformation.*

The story is these countries will one day come to resemble the advanced economies of the U.S., Europe, and Japan, having transitioned along a path of natural development.

The reality is that nothing of the kind is taking place.

The problem with developing countries is this: *they're not developing.*

They're not developing because they've been outmaneuvered by multinational companies.

Most developing countries lack the autonomy to implement industrial policy, or even the regulatory framework they need to develop their own economics.

Instead, they've become pawns in the global system, dependent on foreign investment and granting tax breaks and other concessions to corporations that control it.

Roughly 40 percent of world trade is actually intra-firm trade between affiliates of multinationals.

The largest multinational companies control over half of world trade and some 90 percent of world investment.

The promise of globalization as a driver of development is a fantasy.

That fantasy is promoted by corporate interests and accepted without question as a cornerstone of the bipartisan consensus.

In reality, globalization works to the benefit of Wall Street and global corporations, and to the detriment of democracy and national sovereignty.

Raising World Demand
Low demand is a structural problem of long duration that limits the potential for growth in every country in the world.

The use of low wage labor is the root cause of global trade imbalances that will bring a catastrophic devaluation of the dollar if something isn't done.

Low wages are also the source of excess profits and the explosion of global finance that have destabilized countries throughout the world and will lead to a new Depression without meaningful reform.

Richard Duncan has proposed raising the wages of industrial workers employed in the export sectors of developing countries.

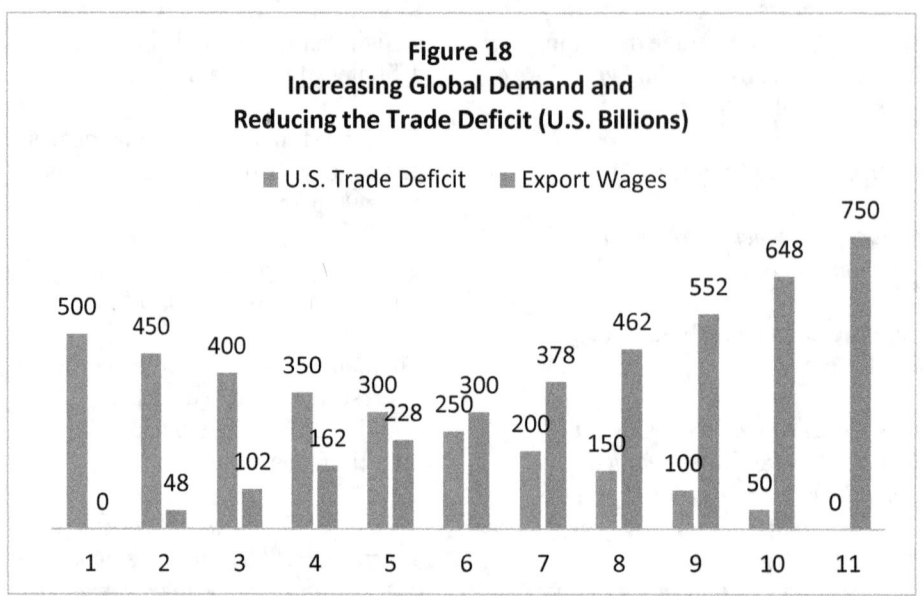

Figure 18
Increasing Global Demand and
Reducing the Trade Deficit (U.S. Billions)

Source: Richard Duncan (2005), The Dollar Crisis: Causes, Consequences, Cures, (New York: John Wiley and Sons), table 12.3, page 242.

Based on an estimated 40 million export workers, raising wages by $1 per day each year over a ten year period would have a dramatic impact on world demand that could eliminate the U.S. trade deficit.

The only way to reduce the U.S. trade deficit is to increase world demand.

Figure 18 shows how raising export wages over ten years, from $5 per day to $15 per day for 40 million workers, would increase demand by $750 billion a year.

That increase in demand could help reduce the trade deficit by $50 billion a year and eliminate the deficit over ten years.

In 2010 the average wage in the Philippines was 31 cents an hour. In 2012 garment workers in Bangladesh earned 18 cents an hour.

There is nothing American industry can produce for low wage markets without consumers.

That's why wage standards are essential to raise demand and increase U.S. exports to bring down the trade deficit.

It is also important to remember the impact of currency devaluations on the dollar equivalent of foreign wages.

In dollar terms, foreign wages fall when foreign currencies are devalued.

For this reason, foreign devaluations have increased the disparity between wages in the U.S. compared to countries throughout Asia and Latin America.

Even so, the magnitude of the wage differential is such that the problem can't be solved by reducing the value of the dollar.

If the dollar falls by 50 percent, the dollar value of foreign wages at $5 a day would rise to $10 a day.

Foreign wages currently at $10 a day would rise in dollar value to $20 a day, equivalent to $2.00 an hour for a ten hour day.

A 50 percent decline in the value of the dollar would be catastrophic for this country, because import prices would rise by 100 percent.

Yet even a decline of this magnitude would not be enough to make American industry competitive in world markets.

At the same time, the pattern of world development has created intense population pressure that works against any natural rise in wages.

The market will only push wages lower over time, while developing country governments have little power to act against global corporations that control that market.

Issues and Implementation

Raising wages of export workers is more practical than trying to raise minimum wages around the world.

It isn't feasible to impose U.S. or European minimum wage rates in developing countries with very low living standards.

But the number of jobs in developing country export sectors only represent one fourth to one third of total employment.

Wages in the wider economy of poor countries would continue to reflect the context of the domestic market, while export wages would eventually reflect consumer wages in the markets where exports are sold.

Duncan's proposal envisions an international agreement to raise export sector wages over time.

While there is nothing wrong with this idea, international agreement is unlikely without support for national initiatives that call for similar standards.

For example, there is no reason for the U.S. to accept the suicidal decline of domestic industry as a side effect of pursing international agreement on wage standards.

I think the U.S. minimum wage should be paid in production or provision of all imported goods and services sold in this country, without exception.

Trade with low wage countries, including those where child labor is a documented practice, has circumvented the minimum wage and child labor laws passed by Congress in 1935.

A U.S. law imposing wage standards on imports would no doubt be in violation of WTO rules. But so what?

China violates WTO rules every day of the year, but the U.S. can't protect itself from unfair wage competition?

The American people do not have to accept this ridiculous and illegitimate double standard.

If we do, historians will one day argue that we got what we deserved.

What about inflation? Wouldn't wage standards drive up import prices in this country?

What is remarkable is how little impact higher wages in poor countries would actually have on import prices.

Multinationals offshore production to other countries based on a range of incentives.

These include low wages and the absence of labor standards, lower health care and benefit costs, lack of health, safety, environmental, and other regulations, and incentives such as tax breaks and subsidies.

Figure 19
Impact of Goods Trade Deficit Reduction ($Billions)
on Manufacturing Employment (Millions)

Annual Goods Deficit:

        Reduce by $400 Billion

Direct Gain in Manufacturing Jobs	Supply Chain Employment	Re-spending Employment
4.0	6.7	4.6

Direct Job Gain:	4.0
Supply Chain Job Gain:	6.7
Re-spending Job Gain:	4.6
Total Employment Gain:	15.3

Source: Josh Bivens, 2003. Updated Employment Multipliers for the U.S. Economy. (Washington, D.C.: Economic Policy Institute). No. 268, Table 8. Based on 1 manufacturing job for every $1.2 million of goods imports. Calculation reflects deduction in job gains from increased productivity.

U.S. multinationals in China also benefit from illegal export subsidies as well as the 40 percent currency subsidy from the under-valued yuan.

The cost of labor is actually a small fraction of total production costs that have been offset by incentives that amount to unfair trade practices.

Given the current state of the U.S. economy, there is very little room for companies to raise prices if they expect to maintain sales.

Instead, wage standards overseas would increase demand and allow U.S. exports to rise.

Increasing U.S. exports would reduce unemployment and raise incomes.

As a result, higher demand in the U.S. and abroad would increase sales for the very companies that oppose wage standards.

This scenario is consistent with principles of the virtuous circle of growth that brought unprecedented prosperity in the post war period.

Re-activating the circle of growth requires a regulatory framework that will benefit private enterprise as it benefits society as a whole.

That framework was based on economic fundamentals that are no different today and point the way to real growth at home and abroad.

What about the sudden and dramatic impact on the world economy U.S. wage standards imposed on imports would have?

Would it be any more sudden and dramatic than closing down manufacturing plants in this country and setting up replacement operations overseas?

Congress could allow a one year time frame for implementation, or phase in standards over a two or three year period.

But it isn't reasonable to tell millions of Americans who are out of work that our political leaders don't have the imagination or the resolve to deal with the issue.

Figure 19 shows the potential impact of reducing the trade deficit in goods.

Reducing the goods trade deficit by 400 billion would recapture 4 million of the 6 million manufacturing jobs lost between 1998 and 2010.

Including the additional jobs gained through supply chains and re-spending effects brings the total gain to more than 15 million jobs.

America simply cannot afford to export manufacturing jobs to foreign countries and the offshore production facilities of U.S. multinationals.

Wage standards are a core principle because low wage labor undermines American industry and limits export markets for American goods.

The American way of life, our standard of living, and the prospects for future generations will rise or fall based on laws that either shield us or fail to protect us from unfair wage competition.

America is the only country in the world that is described as an idea.

As a nation of immigrants, we are descendants of the wider world in terms of ethnicity, race, and national origin.

But America has transcended those origins, and embodies an idea that defines us all.

We are all children of a series of wars, fought in a myriad of ways, to oppose tyranny and the oppression that it spawns.

Low wage labor is not a natural stage of development in the economic transformation of the world.

Rather, it is oppression that brings low wage labor to market, while excess profits become the springboard for tyranny on a global scale.

Excess profits and low wage labor are two sides of the same coin.

We can fight for wage standards, or we can live with the tyranny of Wall Street that threatens to destroy us all.

While repeated stimulus from the Federal Reserve has prevented the onset of deflation and Depression, the current trajectory simply cannot be sustained.

The New Economy model of growth, which relies on debt-based consumption, is no longer viable.

The federal government has continued taking on debt to finance stimulus for consumption.

That policy is necessary, but at best is only a temporary measure.

Viable recovery in consumer demand requires rebuilding the demand generating process in the economy.

That project will require strategic investments needed to transform the consumer economy into a productive economy.

Permanent recovery can only be achieved through revival of the real economy, led by manufacturing and advanced-technology, high-value-added industries.

That means recovery will require reducing the trade deficit and reforming the financial sector to fundamentally restructure the nation's economy.

Main Points

Public investment has been critical to the process of national economic integration.

The federal government provided critical support for railroads in the 19th century, electrical infrastructure in the 1930s, the interstate highway system in the 1950s, and NASA in the 1960s.

There are valid arguments that high long term growth could not have been maintained without large scale government investment in these kinds of projects.

High value-added industry creates high paying jobs.

High wages create demand that attracts investment and generates even more jobs, and so on, in a virtuous circle of growth.

This country has also seen tragic consequences from the lack of government support for industry.

For example, the combined share of world shipbuilding for South Korea, China, and Japan rose from eight percent in 1975, to 86 percent in 2010.

In the 1980s, the U.S. ceded entire industries in consumer electronics to Japanese companies that were being supported by government subsidies.

There has been something of a renaissance in thinking, especially as promoted by the Obama Administration.

But the U.S. still lags far behind in R&D investments.

Between 1995 and 2010, the U.S. traded places with China in a wide range of manufacturing industries.

In 1995, the U.S. out-produced China 7 to 1 in every category.

In 2010, China out-produced the U.S. in every category, and by nearly 2 to 1 in medium high technology industries.

The terms of the debate must change.

The U.S. should invest in new engine technology and biofuels.

Investments should also be made in nanotechnology.

American industry can't compete with foreign rivals that have the advantage of government support.

Strategic investment in high technology industry is essential to support the demand generating process, and re-establish the virtuous circle of growth.

Industrial Policy

Greg Tassey, in a staff paper for the National Institute of Standards and Technology, argues that industrial policy is imperative for long term recovery.

Tassey wrote:
"From 2001-2010, American households increased their debt by $5.7 trillion (75 percent), state and local governments increased their debt by more than $1 trillion (89 percent), and, the federal government increased its debt by $6 trillion (178 percent).

This expansion of domestic demand should have ratcheted up the economy's growth rate. Instead, average annual real GDP growth in this decade was one-third the average for the previous three decades."

Tassey's point goes to the heart of the issue. Government spending to stimulate demand, is not a strategy for long term recovery.

Consider the economic impact of large scale government investment.

Historically this referred to infrastructure such as railroads in the mid to late 19th century, electrical infrastructure like the Hoover Damn and the Tennessee Valley Authority in the 1930s, and the interstate highway system begun in the late 1950s.

There are valid arguments that this country's historic record of growth was due in part to large scale government investment in these kinds of projects.

Currently, the federal government provides direct subsidies over $90 billion per year, and indirect subsidies more than double that figure in key industries such as coal used for electric power.

The question is not whether the U.S. has or will continue to support industrial policy.

The question is whether strategic planning will inform the future direction and extent of investments made to implement that policy.

Consider the unfortunate outcome of government neglect of shipbuilding in this country.

Subsidies were eliminated during the Reagan administration, leaving the industry vulnerable to competition from rivals supported by foreign governments.

In 1975, South Korea, China, and Japan accounted for only 8 percent of world shipbuilding production.

By 2010 these three countries accounted for 86 percent of shipbuilding, while U.S. shipbuilding had fallen to less than 1 percent of world production.

Figure 20
Changes in National R&D Intensity
and Value Added in Manufacturing

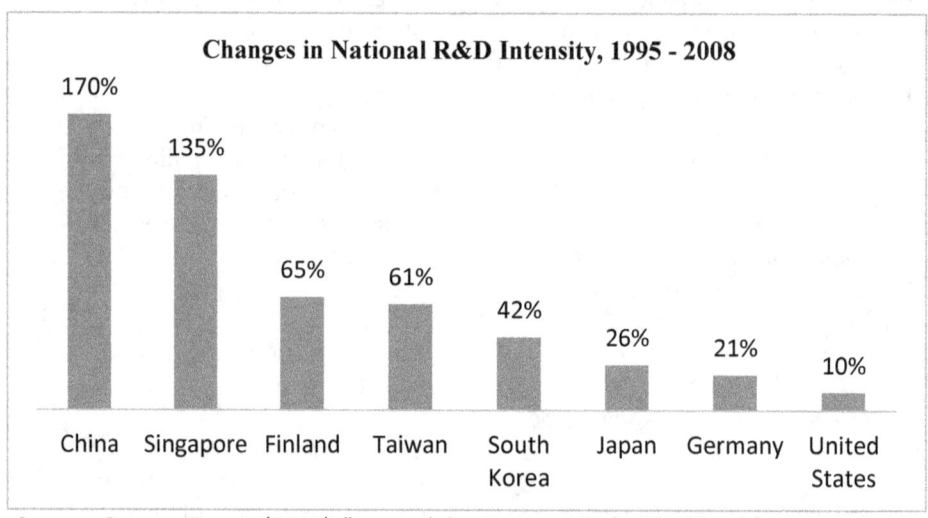

Source: Gregory Tassey (2011), "Beyond the Business Cycle, The Need for a Technology-Based Growth Strategy." Economic Analysis Office, National Institute of Standards and Technology (Washington, D.C.: NIST Economics Staff Paper).

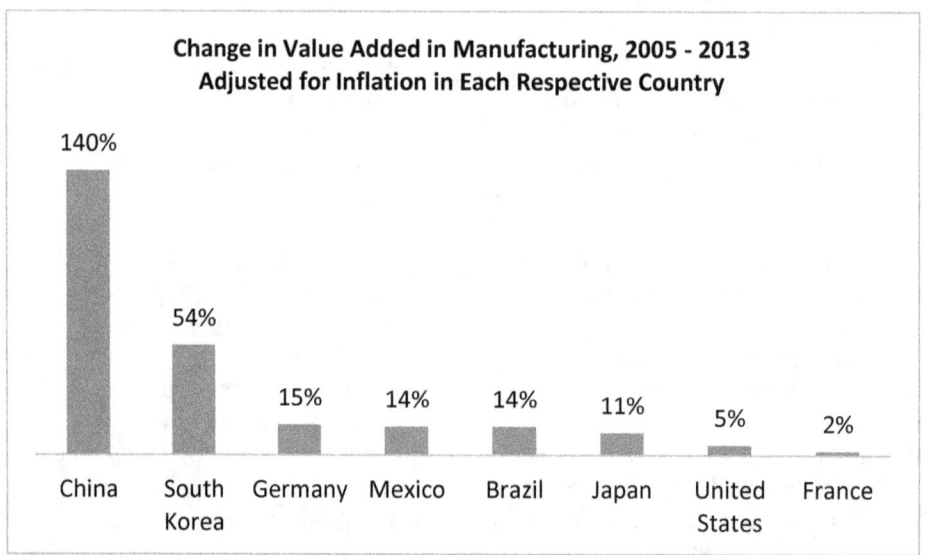

Source: http://unstats.un.org/unsd/snaama/selbasicFast.asp. Shown in Marc Levinson (2015), "U.S. Manufacturing in International Perspective," Congressional Research Service, Washington, D.C., page 6, figure 4.

Alternately, when the U.S. scores a victory, closer examination makes that victory look pale by comparison with foreign rivals.

For example, advanced battery manufacturing has been hailed as a success that brought a production facility to Michigan with the help of then governor Jennifer Granholm.

Even so, consider the investments made by foreign governments for comparison.

For 2007 – 2012 Japan provided $275 million in R&D funding for Li-ion batteries, along with a stated commitment to a 20 year research program.

Germany has provided $1.4 billion over a ten year period for a larger program in automotive electronics, Li-ion batteries, and other applications for vehicles.

China has committed $1.5 trillion to seven key technologies that include alternative energy vehicles.

That program includes the stated goal for China to become the largest producer of Li-ion batteries, projected between 2015 and 2020.

As another example, consider the public-private partnerships funded through the Commerce department's Manufacturing Extension Partnership (MEP).

The MEP is a nationwide network with offices in every state that support innovation and process improvements as well as supplier development and assistance in bringing new technologies to market.

The program generates $32 in economic growth for every $1 of federal investment, with $112 million of funding and $3.6 billion in annual sales.

By comparison, the U.K. invests $389 million annually in similar projects, while Japan invests over *2 billion* annually in its counterpart to the MEP network.

As a percent of GDP, the U.K.'s investment is 20 times greater, while Japan's is 54 times greater than the level of U.S. investment.

The National Science Foundation has compiled data on product and process innovations compared to R&D intensity for 17 industries.

As might be expected, the intensity of R&D has been shown to be strongly correlated with the rate of innovation.

Figure 20 shows the change in R&D intensity (1995 – 2008) for the top countries by rank. The U.S. ranks last among the eight countries shown.

Figure 20 also shows the change in manufacturing value added (2005 – 2013). The U.S. ranks 7th out of the eight countries shown.

Compared to only 5 percent growth of value added in the U.S., China's value added grew by 140 percent.

Figure 21

Global Value Added and Value Added in High Tech Manufacturing

Global Value Added ($Billions)
by Manufacturing Technology Level

	1995	2000	2006	2010	Value added Loss or Gain 2010 % vs. 1995 %
Medium high					
Global Value Added	$1,527	$1,460	$2,114	$2,897	
U.S. Share	21.7%	25.5%	18.8%	14.4%	($211.48)
China Share	2.8%	4.6%	12.2%	26.0%	$672.10
Medium low					
Global Value Added	$1,366	$1,328	$2,199	$2,983	
U.S. Share	19.4%	24.5%	21.7%	17.6%	($53.69)
China Share	3.4%	4.2%	10.0%	19.7%	$486.23
Low					
Global Value Added	$815	$760	$968	$1,221	
U.S. Share	24.8%	30.5%	24.5%	18.6%	($75.70)
China Share	3.3%	5.1%	14.2%	27.7%	$297.92

U.S. 2010 Loss:	($340.88)
China 2010 Gain:	$1,456.26
U.S. 2010 Non-Petroleum Goods Trade Balance:	($369.66)

Source: Natiional Science Board, Science and Engineering Indicators, chapter 6, page 6-27, table 6-A, National Science Foundation, Washington, D.C., 2012.

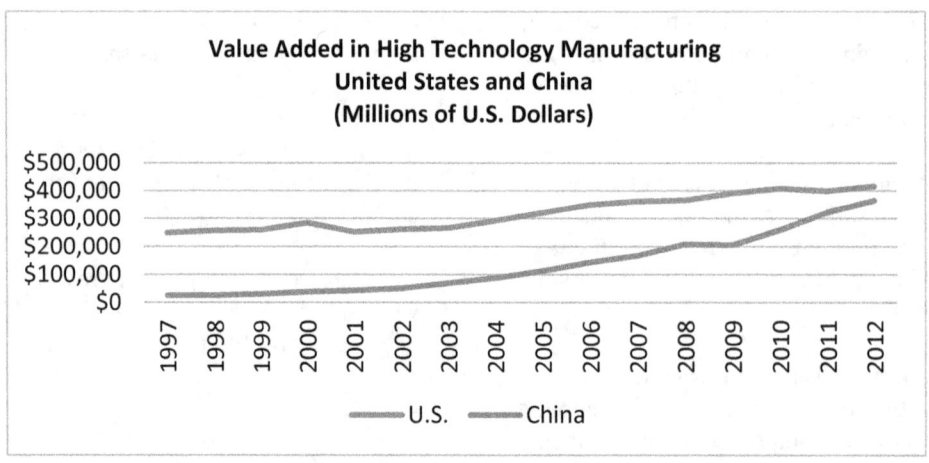

SOURCE: IHS Global Insight, special tabulations (2013) of the World Industry Service database.
Source: Natiional Science Board, Science and Engineering Indicators 2014, Appendix table 6-7, National Science Foundation, Washington, D.C., 2014.

Changing course is critical to America's future in the world economy.

Manufacturing has more value added and more productivity than any other sector.

High technology has the highest productivity of all, and is essential for long term growth.

Policymakers around the world recognize the key role of knowledge-intensive and technology-intensive (KTI) industries in economic growth and national competitiveness.

These industries in both the manufacturing and service sectors lead the development of technological infrastructure that can transform the economy.

For example, information and communications technology (ICT) is considered critical technology infrastructure that serves as a platform on which the economy operates.

Due to the shift toward knowledge and technology intensive production methods, ICT infrastructure is critical to remaining economically competitive.

Figure 21 shows global value added in manufacturing, categorized in three groups according to the level of technology involved in manufacturing.

Production in this country accounted for $340 billion less value in 2010 than would have been created if the 1995 share had been maintained.

In contrast, China's 2010 share accounted for over $1.4 trillion more than would have been created if China's share of global value added had remained at 1995 levels.

Figure 21 also shows China has been rapidly overtaking the U.S. in value added in high tech manufacturing, which for China nearly doubled between 2009 and 2012.

In late 2008 and early 2009 the U.S. committed $67 billion for energy efficiency, renewable energy, transportation, and smart grid technology.

In the same period, China committed $47 billion for energy efficiency, clean vehicles, grid infrastructure, and other energy technologies.

Figure 22
New Investment in
<u>Clean Energy Technology</u>

		2004	2006	2008	2010
China					
	Wind	220	3,678	17,368	44,875
	Solar	3	562	1,981	3,856
	Biofuels	17	1,117	187	N/A
European Union					
	Wind	6,728	12,413	22,546	19,243
	Solar	319	5,359	22,200	11,491
	Biofuels	477	4,450	1,994	167
United States					
	Wind	1,574	9,210	17,593	17,142
	Solar	153	2,389	7,834	5,580
	Biofuels	989	10,448	4,078	1,155

Source: Natiional Science Board, Science and Engineering Indicators,
chapter 6, page 6-64, table 6-12, National Science Foundation,
Washington, D.C., 2012.

Private investment in clean energy technologies, by selected region/country/economy: 2004–14

(Billions of dollars)

Year	United States	China	EU	Japan	ROW
2004	5.4	2.4	20.8	4.0	8.9
2005	11.7	7.4	31.6	4.0	15.5
2006	29.5	10.3	42.4	3.2	24.2
2007	35.5	15.7	62.4	2.7	37.3
2008	37.5	24.8	76.1	3.4	39.8
2009	26.8	38.7	73.4	5.3	35.1
2010	41.6	40.8	105.0	7.9	50.2
2011	56.8	50.5	114.8	10.8	55.0
2012	43.7	64.4	81.7	18.5	56.4
2013	40.0	64.8	50.6	32.6	51.6
2014	43.4	86.3	49.5	36.9	64.9

EU = European Union; ROW = rest of world. Clean energy technologies include biomass,
geothermal, wind, solar, biofuels, and energy smart and efficiency technologies.
Private investment includes asset finance, small distributed capacity, venture capital,
private equity, reinvested equity, and public markets. Mergers and acquisitions are
excluded. Source: Bloom New Energy Finance, http://bnef.com/, special tabluations:
Source: National Science Board, Science and Engineering Indicators 2016,
chapter 6, figure 6-47, National Science Foundation, Washington, D.C., 2016.

Figure 22 shows new investment in wind, solar, and biofuels. New U.S. investment in wind energy was a little more than a third of new China investment of $45 billion in 2010.

In 2014, U.S. investment of $43 billion in clean energy technologies was only half of China's $86 billion investment.

In this country policy space is restricted by the political debate over the budget.

In 2012, the choice presented to the public was between a candidate who spent $90 billion over two years on clean energy, and a candidate who ridiculed that expenditure.

The terms of the debate are misleading, because it provides the public with limited choices that make little reference to the context of international competition.

Instead, it is clearly more accurate to define the choice as whether or not to keep pace with China or European countries for example, in funding investments in wind energy and solar energy technology.

New Engine Technology and Biofuels
Developed in 2004, revolutionary Cyclone Power engines are currently in use as tank engines in a pilot program for the U.S. Army.

They can be scaled down for use as lawn mower engines, or scaled up for use in long haul trucking, railway locomotives, and maritime shipping.

The Cyclone Power engine is an advanced steam engine that can replace the internal combustion engine altogether.

Cyclone Power engine features include:
- Multi-Fuel - Will burn any combustible fuel including biomass and municipal waste
- Clean burning with any fuel – Provides complete combustion and a very clean exhaust
- Non-polluting when using biofuels
- Provides an ideal power source for hybrid and conventional vehicles.
- Mileage comparable to diesels on the highway, and far better in city traffic
- De-ionized water used for engine lubrication, so no oil of any kind is required
- No radiator, water pump, oil pump, fuel injection, or catalytic converter required
- Two speed transmission for most vehicles, with far simpler design than transmissions now in use
- Better torque compared to conventional engines
- Low noise, Low vibration due to simpler and more efficient engine design
- Fewer moving parts and much longer engine life compared to gasoline or diesel engines
- Lower weight and simpler design is less expensive to produce than conventional engines.

Cyclone Power engines can run on any combustible fuel, but don't require any oil or petroleum based fuel or lubricants of any kind.

There is also far less need for refinement of biofuels like ethanol or biodiesel, with potential cost reduction of 30 percent or more in the cost of biofuel production.

That translates to a cost of around $2.50 per gallon for plant-based biodiesel, which doesn't need to be blended with regular diesel or any kind of alcohol or petroleum based fuel.

Use of biofuels would also result in a zero carbon footprint.

Carbon dioxide emitted by plants used for biodiesel is removed from the environment, while the carbon dioxide exhaust from Cyclone engines would replace it.

By eliminating petroleum as a fuel, the use of Cyclone engines would have an enormous impact on global warming.

Anyone who doubts how much damage global warming can cause should talk to residents of New Orleans, New York, and New Jersey.

Current projections are that sea level will rise by 2 feet in the next hundred years, based on using fossil fuels for energy.

In this country there are roughly 250 million passenger cars on the road, with new car sales in 2015 recorded at over 18 million.

Using progressive adoption in increments of 5 per cent each year, half of all new vehicles sold could be powered by the new engines within 10 years.

Roughly 40 percent of the U.S. trade deficit is due to oil imports, which could be cut in half over the next ten years.

The price of oil would fall dramatically once the program was announced, as projected profits from oil production would be significantly reduced by 2025.

Prices for gas and diesel could fall by $1.50 to $2.00 a gallon, and reduce the U.S. trade deficit in petroleum.

In 2014 the U.S. ran a trade deficit in petroleum of $190 billion dollars.

Re-directing that spending to biofuels would mean eliminating the oil deficit, eliminating the corresponding leakage from the economy, and boosting domestic demand.

The total economic impact would be even greater, because outside the U.S. there are another 750 million cars on the road world-wide.

Global warming is a global problem.

Any chance we have to stop or significantly slow the rise in sea level will require cutting the use of fossil fuels on a global basis.

We have existing technology in this country that can be used to address the world's most pressing environmental issue and transform the U.S. economy at the same time.

There are also numerous advantages over electric vehicles, such as range, power, and the fact there would be no need for extensive investment in electrical grid infrastructure.

The aftermath of hurricanes and winter storms also illustrate the vulnerability of relying on electricity for power generally, which would be even worse for transportation.

The obstacles for adopting non-polluting Cyclone engines are not technological, but political.

The vested interests are automakers that don't own and can't control the technology.

Investment of $1 trillion to $2 trillion dollars over the next ten years could transform the global economy and guarantee the pre-eminent position of the U.S. as a world power.

The U.S. could become the world's top producer of clean engine technology and top exporter of vehicle engines over the next five to ten years.

While the program would pay for itself and transform the U.S. economy, the fall in oil prices worldwide would also increase world demand for other products, including U.S. exports.

Public-private partnerships could also raise private investment to finance the project and give U.S. oil companies a stake in the process.

Conversion to clean energy would also reduce the need for military spending, as U.S. dependence on Mid-East oil would be eliminated.

Whatever reliance that remains on fossil fuels such as natural gas could be provided by domestic suppliers.

The only caveat is that government investment should be conditioned on agreement not to outsource production.

With that provision, non-polluting engines and affordable biofuels could make this country energy independent and eliminate the U.S. trade deficit.

Replacing the global fleet with clean engine vehicles would create millions of jobs in this country, while spending re-directed to the domestic economy would create even more jobs.

This kind of investment is a no-brainer, and there is no excuse for anyone to argue some ideological position to oppose it.

We can change the world and build long term job security for the future at the same time.

I think most people would rather have a job than an ideological position, any day of the week.

Nanotechnology

Investments should also be made in revolutionary technologies to facilitate the development of solar energy as well as other industrial processes.

Nanotechnology involves the development of materials on a molecular level that have a wide range of applications.

For example, development of new materials will revolutionize the next generation of electric cars.

Nanotechnology will be used to produce high capacity batteries, fuel-based catalytic range extenders, electric motors, smart silicon and thin-film solar panels, advanced sensors and electronics, and lightweight composites for vehicles.

One such material is graphene.

Graphene is the strongest material known to science and can be produced in sheets as thin as an atom that are better at conducting electricity than copper.

The potential for graphene includes development of materials used as clothing with embedded digitized processing.

Credit cards could evolve to hold as much processing power as today's smartphone.

A Rice University professor described the potential of graphene by stating "You could theoretically roll up your iPhone and stick it behind your ear like a pencil."

There is no reason for the U.S. to allow other countries to take the lead in developing these kinds of next generation technologies.

The National Nanotechnology Initiative was launched in 2000 under the George W. Bush administration and receives funding through a variety of public-private partnerships.

Annual funding in this country is currently less than $2 billion, roughly on par with investments being made in China.

Considering the potential magnitude of economic impact, the U.S. should invest $500 billion dollars over the next ten years to become the undisputed world leader in nanotechnology.

Investment on this scale would transform the U.S. economy and put America at the forefront of what will become the next industrial revolution.

Funding Strategic Investments
With U.S. debt currently at $19 trillion, what impact would there be of an additional $3 trillion in debt used to finance these strategic investments?

U.S. debt will rise regardless of whether we continue to rely on government stimulus for consumption, or whether we make investments that could transform the economy and bring a new century of economic growth.

Government debt in Japan rose from 70 percent of GDP in 1990 to 230 percent of GDP in 2012.

There are important differences between the U.S. and Japan, because the bulk of Japan's debt is owed to the country's citizens, not foreigners.

The U.S. has a much higher proportion of debt owed to foreigners, which makes the country far more vulnerable to financial markets.

Even so, the point is that very high levels of debt can be maintained, provided there is no loss of confidence on the part of creditors that the debt will be repaid.

For the U.S., it's clear the continued accumulation of debt for consumption will ultimately lead to a crisis of confidence.

The reason is precisely that the U.S. is not making the investments that will generate the level of growth required to pay down the debt over time.

As a practical matter, there may be no viable alternative.

Growth based on next generation technologies is required to generate the wealth we need to pay down the debt and prosper in the 21st century.

The U.S. can currently borrow money at 2 percent interest, which may continue to be the case over the next four to five years.

But if borrowing continues as a means to finance stimulus for consumption, rates could easily double or triple in a relatively short period of time.

Austerity is not an option, unless we accept long term deflation that may be impossible to reverse once it begins.

Perpetuating the status quo will also lead ultimately to a catastrophic outcome.

Currently there is no end in sight to continued stagnation, stimulus, and even the potential for future bailouts.

While strategic investment is an imperative for recovery and long term growth, SWIFT Act proposals include raising revenue through a value added tax and a tax on financial transactions.

Regardless of how programs are funded, large scale investment in manufacturing is no longer an option.

The only way to pay down the debt is to grow the tax base through revival of American industry.

The only chance of permanent recovery is to engage the new industrial revolution this country can either lead or choose to cede to foreign rivals.

We can face reality or we can pursue the illusion that we have any viable alternative.

Financial Reform

Main Points

The financial crisis created a mandate for reform.

The central legislation was the Dodd-Frank Act, passed by Congress in 2009.

Dodd-Frank left the details to regulators, which allowed lobbyists and legal challenges that have delayed implementation and thwarted the original intent of the law.

The essential mandate falls in three areas:

First, reduce systemic risk, by imposing limits on leverage and requiring separation between commercial banks and investment firms.

Second, the financial sector should be subject to taxes designed to establish parity between returns from financial investment and the investments needed in productive industry.

There is no chance of restoring productive investment in American industry, without addressing the enormous profits generated by financial investments.

Third, compensating CEOs with stock options should be prohibited.

Nothing has done more harm than the practice of paying CEOs to liquidate companies to drive up stock prices.

Revival of American industry requires bringing an end to stock incentives that make offshoring profitable for CEOs.

Fourth, the Consumer Financial Protection Bureau should establish a voluntary pension fund for private sector employees.

The impact would save $3 billion a year currently paid in fees to Wall Street, and potentially raise retirement income by some $300 billion a year.

The financial crisis created a mandate to create transparency and reduce leverage by imposing reserve requirements.

The language of the Dodd-Frank Act was intended to limit speculation and reduce the potential for systemic risk when banks fail, as well as provide mechanisms to prevent future bailouts.

Delays in implementing Dodd-Frank have allowed the banks to continue speculating in derivatives, while calls for immediate reform have gained increasing bipartisan support.

While Dodd-Frank was passed into law in July 2010, details of how various provisions would be implemented were left open for regulatory agencies to establish.

The result has been a concerted lobbying effort as well as legal challenges designed to undermine the original intent of the law and the power of agencies to enforce key aspects of the regulations involved.

For example, along with establishing federal insurance on deposits, Glass-Steagall prohibited securities trading for banks and their affiliates.

The Dodd-Frank counterpart is the Volcker rule, which prevents banks from engaging in so-called proprietary trading that does not benefit customers.

When a bank trades on its own (proprietary) account, the bank is in essence trading on its own behalf with federally insured customer deposits.

Yet the Volcker rule is widely considered inadequate as a substitute for outright prohibition on bank trading in securities.

Due to unprecedented lobbying by the financial sector, the Volcker rule was further weakened by exemptions before final passage in 2014.

Another example was the move by Bank of America in October 2011 to transfer $53 trillion in derivatives from its Merrill Lynch affiliate to the bank side of the company, which is insured by the FDIC.

The transfer was made in response to lowering of Moody's credit rating, which naturally was lower for Merrill Lynch Securities than for the federally insured Bank of America parent that owns Merrill.

If the derivatives transfer had been blocked, Bank of America would have been required to put up an additional $3.2 billion in collateral due to the lower credit rating.

Bank of America 3Q2011 profits were $6.2 billion, so the additional capital would have been equivalent to a little more than half the profits from one quarter.

The FDIC opposed the move, which transfers a level of risk the agency has no way of insuring.

For example, a loss of 10 percent on the $53 trillion derivative face value would amount to an actual loss of $5.3 trillion.

The derivatives transferred were 71 percent of the $75 trillion total held by Bank of America at the time.

By comparison, JPMorgan Chase is FDIC insured and holds 99 percent of the company's total $79 trillion in derivatives.

The legal context is Section 23A of the Federal Reserve Act, designed to prevent non-bank affiliates from benefitting from access to the Fed discount window and FDIC insurance on deposits.

The Fed had previously granted exemptions to both Bank of America and JPMorgan Chase, making derivatives trading by these retail banks legal for the time being.

The controversy in the Bank of America case was due to both the value of the transfer involved, and the ongoing delay in implementing Dodd-Frank that limits bank trading in derivatives.

In the aftermath of subsequent disclosure of $6 billion in losses by JPMorgan, Senate candidate Elizabeth Warren renewed calls to reinstate Glass-Steagall.

Reinstating Glass-Steagall was originally proposed in July 2010 by Republican Senator John McCain and Democrat Senator Maria Cantwell.

After the initiative failed to pass the Senate, a House version was introduced in July 2011 by Democrat Representative Maurice Hinchey.

Supporters point out Glass-Steagall was only 37 pages long, and was the basis for financial stability for nearly 60 years until it was overturned during the Clinton administration.

Reinstating Glass-Steagall would prevent crises in the trading markets from impacting the stability of retail banking that provides credit to businesses and households.

For example, the 1987 crash of the stock market had little effect on the banks, which at that time were barred from trading or owning securities firms as affiliates.

Reinstatement would require the banks to sell off non-bank affiliates, which includes securities traders as well as insurance companies like Travelers owned by Citigroup.

Goldman Sachs is a securities firm that became a bank holding company for the specific purpose of gaining FDIC insurance and access to the Fed discount window.

Glass-Steagall would require revocation of Goldman's status for continued operation as a securities trader.

Former president Clinton has described the repeal of Glass-Steagall as a mistake.

Expressions of support for reinstatement have also come from Republicans, including former House Speaker Newt Gingrich and Vice Presidential candidate Paul Ryan during the 2012 Republican primary.

Other conservative support has centered on a more extensive break-up of the banks than Glass-Steagall requires.

Seven years after the 2008 financial crisis, unregulated trading in derivatives continues, because nothing has been done to stop it.

The banks are as much at risk of collapse today as they were in 2008.

Worse still, the federal government today is far more entangled with the banks, and has greater explicit liability for their losses, than before the crisis.

There are two immediate and inter-related problems.

Simon Johnson, a former chief economist for the IMF, wrote in 2009 that banks were hiding the extent of losses on toxic assets, and hoarding cash instead of making loans.

Revealing the full extent of losses would mean acknowledging that liabilities exceed the value of bank assets.

When banks try to down play how bad things really are, the economy suffers from the lack of lending.

As we've seen, the banks continue to gamble in speculative markets, hoping for big profits to offset their losses.

Consider the $2 billion in losses announced by J.P. Morgan in May 2012, which were revised upward first to $3 billion and then within a month to nearly $6 billion dollars.

Those losses exposed gambling that took place with federally insured deposits.

Johnson has consistently made the case that the banks pose systemic risk by virtue of being too big and having too much leverage based on too little equity required for reserves.

Johnson considers the only solution to be federal intervention to oversee bankruptcy for troubled banks.

Toxic assets would be written down to their true value and transferred to a separate trust designated to sell them off to the public.

The banks involved could then be sold back to the private sector, to resume lending without the burden of toxic assets.

Unfortunately, the Federal Reserve has bypassed Johnson's proposal, by purchasing toxic mortgages, not at market value, but at the bank's recorded book value of the original loan.

Then the Bank of International Settlements (BIS) decided to allow banks to change the classification of non-performing loans, so that on paper they have the same value as performing loans.

In essence, the BIS rule means a mortgage is a bank asset, regardless of whether anybody pays the monthly note.

The Federal Reserve not only accepted that change, but then began paying the banks interest on the bad mortgages the Fed already bought and paid for.

The Fed has bailed out the banks, to the tune of $75 billion a month in 2013 and $30 billion a month in 2014.

The Fed now owns $4.5 trillion of toxic assets and U.S. government debt.

The premise for what the Fed has done is that the market will eventually recover.

But if there is a loss of confidence in the international reserve value of the dollar, not only the banks but the U.S. Treasury and the Federal Reserve would go bankrupt.

Clearly, the over-riding problem is the size of the banks involved, making them too big to fail without undermining the stability of the entire system.

The solution is to break up the banks into separate lines of business and impose size limitations. Regional operating restrictions should also be imposed.

Conservative support for breaking up the banks has come from John Huntsman during the 2012 Republican primary, James Pethokoukis of the American Enterprise Institute, and former Reagan budget chief David Stockman.

In May 2012 U.S. Sen. Sherrod Brown (D-OH) re-introduced the Safe, Accountable, Fair & Efficient (SAFE) Banking Act designed to prevent bailouts by imposing size limits.

The SAFE Banking Act:

- Imposes a strict 10 percent cap on any bank's share of the total amount of deposits of all insured banks in the U.S. This would eliminate loopholes in the existing statutory cap.
- Imposes a strict 10 percent cap on the liabilities that any one financial company can take on, relative to the U.S. financial sector. Like the deposit concentration limit, this closes loopholes in existing law.
- Imposes a limit on the non-deposit liabilities (including off-balance-sheet (OBS) exposure) of a bank holding company of 2 percent of GDP. No bank holding company could exceed $1.3 trillion.
- Imposes a limit on the non-deposit liabilities (including OBS exposure) of any non-bank financial institution of 3 percent of GDP.
- Codifies a 10 percent leverage limit (including OBS exposure) for large bank holding companies and selected nonbank financial institutions into law.

The Act was supported by former Federal Reserve chairman Paul Volcker and ranking Republican Senate Banking Committee member Richard Shelby.

Other supporters included former Bush appointed chair of the FDIC Sheila Bair, and Thomas Hoenig, FDIC board member and former president of the Kansas City Federal Reserve.

Others included four current Federal Reserve Bank presidents – Richard Fisher of Dallas, Esther George of Kansas City, Charles Plosser of Philadelphia, and Jeffrey Lacker of Richmond.

After the Act failed to pass, Senators John McCain (R-AZ) and Elizabeth Warren (D-MA) introduced the 21st Century Glass-Steagall Act in the 113th Congress (2014-2015).

Warren and McCain reintroduced the bill in the 114th Congress (2015-2016), and were joined by Bernie Sanders (I-Vermont), Angus King (I-ME), and Maria Cantwell (D-WA).

The SAFE Banking Act (SAFE) includes all of the key provisions of Glass-Steagall, but also imposes size limitations.

While Glass-Steagall would force banks to sell their interest in brokerage firms, SAFE would also limit the size of the banks themselves.

While the top 20 banks control 90 percent of U.S. assets, the six largest banks control $9.6 trillion in assets equal to 64 percent GDP.

Bloomberg estimates the banks received $7.8 trillion in loans and guarantees from the Federal Reserve following the 2008 crisis.

Partly as a result, federal government debt held by the public went from 36 percent of GDP in 2007 to 73 percent of GDP in 2012, more than doubling in less than five years.

Financial Transactions Tax
After the 1987 stock market crash both president Bush (senior) and Republican Senate Majority leader Bob Dole called for a financial speculation tax to limit volatility in the market.

More than 40 countries tax financial transactions, more commonly referred to as financial transactions tax (FTT).

There has also been recent discussion among the member countries of the European Union about a uniform tax on transactions to curb speculation.

What would not be affected:
- ATM withdrawals
- Mortgages when issued to property buyer
- Other non-mortgage loans
- Short term revolving loans or credit lines
- Initial issues of stocks or bonds
- 401(k) or mutual fund account transactions

What would be affected:
- Stocks
- Securities
- Debt instruments in the secondary market
- Options
- Credit default swaps
- Foreign Exchange (FOREX) trades
- Derivatives

Taxing financial transactions such as these would have minimal impact on long term investments but could significantly curb speculation.

Some 85 percent of taxable trades are carried out between banks and other financial institutions such as hedge funds.

The general public is not involved in trading assets like bonds or derivatives.

In addition to curbing high frequency trading, an FTT could also close loopholes that have been lobbied into Dodd-Frank regulations.

Under most FTT systems, the tax is required as a stamp duty on the transfer of contract ownership.

If a transfer has not been "stamped" as tax compliant, there is no legal transfer of title.

Because contracts without legal title are not enforceable, there is little incentive to avoid payment of the tax.

Tax compliance is also required by clearing houses for trading on regulated exchanges.

The FTT is a particularly effective form of tax as a requirement for legal transfer of title.

The effectiveness of any mechanism for reform depends on how its' enforced and the extent of exemptions from regulation.

For example, consider the Dodd-Frank exemption on derivatives trading for firms handling less than $8 billion a year in transactions.

An FTT would reduce the impact of exemptions, because the value of contracts being traded would be reported in the process of tax collection.

The only way to get around an FTT would be to exempt certain traders from the tax.

While lobbyists will certainly try, it could be far more difficult to win support for tax exemption as being a legitimate exception to regulations.

A similar case was Treasury Secretary Geithner's exemption for trades on the foreign exchange (FOREX) market.

In 2010 Geithner stated in Senate testimony that in his view the FOREX market didn't need to be regulated.

Yet from the time Lehman Brothers collapsed in September 2008 through 2009, the Federal Reserve pumped $5.4 trillion into currency exchanges to prevent their collapse.

This bail out of the FOREX market only became known after passage of the Sanders Amendment to Dodd-Frank, which required detailed disclosure by the Fed on its financial operations.

As with the issue of breaking up the banks, Geithner's position was both revealing and disturbing as a clear example of collusion with the financial lobby and opposition to meaningful reform.

Here again, an FTT could reduce the impact of FOREX exemptions from regulation, unless opponents win exemptions from the tax.

An FTT proposed by the European Union would be based on tax residence.

In this country this would mean any business or individual registered as a U.S. taxpayer would be subject to the tax, wherever in the world the asset is traded.

Geithner's FOREX exemption (officially passed in 2012) leaves a lack of transparency in that $4 trillion a day market in place.

An FTT would at least require reporting the value and type of contracts being traded for the purpose of tax collection.

As with trading in the derivatives market overall, high frequency FOREX trading would be most directly impacted.

It has been estimated that speculation accounts for 80 to 90 percent of FOREX trading, with only the remainder having any contribution to the real economy.

In 2011 Congressional Democrats introduced the Wall Street Trading and Speculators Tax Act, which would impose a tax of 0.03 percent on financial transactions.

The problem with this level of tax is that it wouldn't be high enough to have a significant impact on speculation.

Analysis of an FTT set at 0.5 percent on stock trades and scaled for different types of instruments would be far more effective.

Based on a reduction in trading volume of 50 percent, an FTT of 0.5 percent would raise an estimated one percent of GDP, with the projected equivalent at $180 billion a year in 2015.

The point of levying an FTT, aside from raising revenue, is to reduce the profitability of the financial sector overall.

In 2014 after tax profits of the financial sector were nearly as high as before the 2008 crisis.

In 2Q2015 banks posted profits of $43 billion, passing record levels set in 2013.

Productive (job creating) investment will never recover as long as financial investment is vastly more profitable.

Imposing an FTT would reduce system risk by curbing speculation and free up capital for productive investment.

Tax revenues could also be used to finance public investments in new technologies.

In summary, FTT benefits include:
- Reducing systemic risk from speculation
- Reducing the impact of regulatory exemptions
- Encouraging private sector productive investments
- Financing strategic government investments

Prohibit Granting Stock Options

In the early 2000s there were epic scandals in the collapse and bankruptcy of companies like Enron, Global Crossing, and World Com.

The headlines were filled with criminal prosecution of top executives and accounting firms like Arthur Anderson.

The response in 2002 was passage of a financial reform bill known as Sarbanes-Oxley.

Sarbanes-Oxley imposed disclosure requirements and created an Accounting Oversight Board to review company financial records and prevent fraudulent reporting.

And as discussed in Volume 2, in 2004 the FASB passed its rule that requires companies to disclose the expense of stock options in their financial statements.

Essentially, Sarbanes-Oxley and the FASB rule were intended to re-assure the markets, by imposing standards for integrity in financial reporting.

Yet, as important as these measures were, the underlying problem was never addressed.

The underlying problem is the practice of granting stock options to CEOs and other top executives.

Stock options are the corner stone of promoting *shareholder value*, because they guarantee management will pursue high stock prices.

As we've seen, this has been the mechanism whereby financial interests gained control over American business.

The process has created enormous wealth for Wall Street and U.S. multinationals, at the expense of American industry.

Stock options promote offshoring, because companies that move manufacturing overseas have larger profits, and hence higher stock values.

The logical conclusion is that executive compensation with stock options should be outlawed.

It is beyond unacceptable that offshoring is promoted by Wall Street and by CEOs who are paid hundreds of millions of dollars to move production to low wage countries.

There was also nothing in Sarbanes-Oxley that prevented collusion between the banks and the ratings agencies that created the 2008 financial crisis.

SWIFT Act proposals would prohibit granting stock options to corporate executives and board members.

What is undeniable is that bipartisan support in Washington has endorsed the annihilation of American industry.

We will change the Wall Street rules that have deindustrialized America, or we will cease to exist as an industrial power.

Pension Reform

In 1999, corporate lobbying efforts won a rule change from the labor department that governed the treatment of pension fund balances in corporate accounting.

The effect was to lift restrictions on withdrawals, and allow the use of pensions to finance company operations.

By 2006, *more than 18,000 companies* had underfunded employee pension plans, creating a combined deficit of $450 billion dollars.

Employees were also shifted to defined contribution 401(k) retirement plans, which pay far less in benefits than do pensions.

In the 1980s, mutual funds marketed the lower cost of 401(k) plans as a boon to companies, while stressing the higher returns on investment for employees.

But the retirement value of a 401(k) plan is typically far less than a comparable pension plan.

As shown in Volume 2, many employees in 401(k) plans receive monthly benefits worth only 25 percent of pension benefits that were the norm for the previous generation.

In 2006 and 2012, pension reform bills imposed audit requirements and limited what companies can do with their pension funds.

Yet, the underlying problem wasn't addressed.

The underlying problem is that our politicians (who themselves have pensions) promote the idea that 401(k) plans are a viable alternative to a company pension.

For the overwhelming majority, the prospect of retirement based on social security and a 401(k) plan, is daunting.

It is beyond unacceptable that the public should be expected to depend on the stock market for retirement.

Pensions have been shown to be far more cost effective (lower contributions generate higher benefits), than 401(k) plans.

Private sector employees need pension plans that don't disappear every time they change jobs.

The logical conclusion is that the problem can't be left to employers to solve.

The Consumer Financial Protection Bureau (CFPB) is an independent agency responsible for consumer protection in the financial sector.

The CFPB could administer a voluntary pension plan for private sector employees who want a reliable way to build security for retirement.

While funding would be provided by contributions from both employers and employees, the current penalties faced by short term employees would be eliminated.

Pensions are designed to maximize the benefits of large pools of people participating in the plans over a long period.

Long term employment was the norm when the economy was based on manufacturing.

But today the economy is based on finance, and short term employment has become the norm.

It doesn't make sense to penalize people in the workforce for changes in the job market that are beyond their control.

Government policy has been the driving force behind the change, and the federal government should take responsibility for the problems it has played such a central role in creating.

The CFPB could administer a private employee pension plan, and give every working person the same retirement security that was the norm for the previous generation.

There is one obstacle that poses a serious challenge.

The problem is that 401(k) plans generate *$3 billion dollars a year* in fees for Wall Street.

That's why the only option available to some 70 percent of employees is the 401(k).

Between 2013 and 2014, median household income for those 65 and older declined by 2.7 percent, to just under $37,000.

As more people reach retirement age with inadequate resources in their 401(k) plans, income for that age group will go down.

With the Census Bureau reporting more than 46 million people age 65 and above, the implications for the economy are sobering.

For example, if for that age group median household income rose to $47,000, the impact would create much more demand than would median income at $37,000.

Based on 30 million households, a difference of $10,000 per household would add an additional $300 billion a year in median income.

Boosting consumer demand by some $300 billion a year would have a dramatic impact on the economy overall.

The question to consider is what value there is to the larger economy, for retirement savings in 401(k) plans to generate $3 billion a year in fees for Wall Street?

The reality is that the system currently in place creates a drag on the economy that we can't afford to ignore.

For a real economy business, profits are based on sales. But businesses can't make sales to low income households.

So if you think raising retirement income is about feeling sorry for people, you're missing the point.

The only way to create jobs is to make it profitable for real economy companies to do business in America.

The way to ensure that result is to re-establish a market of high income consumers.

The fact is, income distribution impacts the economy, and excess profits on Wall Street undermine demand.

Excess profits create millionaire incomes for a small group of people who are sucking the economy dry.

That's why SWIFT Act proposals include establishing a private employee pension system administered by the CFPB.

We can unite in common cause and insist on reform, or we can all live with the consequences of letting Wall Street run our country into the ground.

Main Points

In 2009 a trade reform bill entitled The TRADE Act was prevented from being offered for a vote in either house of Congress.

Instead, in 2011 Congress passed trade agreements with Korea, Columbia, and Panama that were endorsed by President Obama.

In 2015 a phony reform bill entitled "The TRADE Act of 2015" was introduced to pass the Trans Pacific Partnership (TPP).

The TPP has been called a new "NAFTA for the Pacific," and will primarily benefit China.

Other reform legislation has also failed to pass.

Proposals to end tax deferral on overseas profits, and to give tax credits equal to 20 percent of the cost of moving overseas jobs back to the United States, were defeated.

A failed reform bill to penalize China for currency manipulation was not supported by the Obama Whitehouse, and was opposed by then Treasury Secretary Tim Geithner.

While these reform bills have received bipartisan support, the equally bipartisan opposition has had overwhelming victory and defeated every proposal.

There has been bipartisan consideration of a value added tax (VAT), which would tax imports but provide a tax rebate for exports.

The result would be to create an incentive for companies to produce in this country instead of overseas.

Trade and Tax Reform

The TRADE Act (Trade, Reform, Accountability, Development and Employment Act) was introduced in 2008 by Senator Sherrod Brown and Representative Mike Michaud.

The goal of the bill was to ensure that provisions in all trade agreements are beneficial for the United States.

If the bill had been enacted it would have required a review of both current and future trade agreements.

This would include a review of the current NAFTA, CAFTA, and WTO agreements, the recently passed agreements with Korea, Columbia, and Panama, and the proposed Trans-Pacific Partnership.

The bill set out standards and dispute remedies to be required in all current and future agreements.

Requirements included labor and environmental standards, food and product safety standards, agriculture rules, and national security exceptions.

The bill also included remedies for currency manipulation and violation of provisions for border tax equity between the U.S. and trade agreement countries.

Equally important, the bill identified provisions that should not be included in trade agreements.

The bill would have prohibited bans on "buy American" provisions, and requires the consent of state governments for procurement, investment, or services provisions contained in any trade agreement.

These are important steps to protect U.S. sovereignty and limit the "fast track" implementation of trade agreements that do not comply with TRADE Act provisions.

The bill was re-introduced in 2009 and gained 148 cosponsors in the House and 9 in the Senate, but stalled in committee and was not submitted for a vote in either chamber.

Instead, in October 2011 Congress passed trade agreements with Korea, Columbia, and Panama endorsed by President Obama.

These trade bills are the clearest example of bipartisan consensus on a globalist ideology that runs counter to both liberal and conservative views in this country.

And now the name of Sherrod Brown's bill has been used for a new bill to pass the Trans Pacific Partnership (TPP).

Brown opposes the "TRADE Act of 2015," passed by Congress in 2015 but which is still pending a vote of ratification sometime in 2016.

The TPP has been called a new "NAFTA for the Pacific," and will do nothing but add to the destruction of American industry.

The U.S. has lost over a million jobs from NAFTA, and over 20 million from unrestricted trade with China.

TPP means offshoring, and is backed by the Wall Street / Trade complex.

Conservative opposition to unrestricted trade was a cornerstone of Ross Perot's candidacy during the 1992 presidential election.

Since then conservatives have consistently argued that low wage labor and abuses of the trading system undermine U.S. manufacturing and damage our economy.

These include Pat Choate (Perot's running mate), Pat Buchanan (Reagan speechwriter and 2000 presidential candidate), Paul Craig Roberts (assistant Secretary of the Treasury under Reagan), and Lou Dobbs (Republican business journalist).

Overwhelming Republican support for the 2011 trade agreements underscores the divide between conservative opposition to unrestricted trade and the free trade philosophy of the Republican party.

See for example The Conservative Caucus Foundation publication, *The Conservative Case Against Free Trade*.

Equally important, support from roughly a third of Democrats in the House and two thirds in Senate was also critical in passing the 2011 trade agreements.

Despite opposition from two thirds of House Democrats, President Obama sent the bills to Congress and secured their passage with bipartisan support.

Other Trade Legislation

A proposal to end tax deferral on overseas profits was included in the Wyden-Coats bill, which would also have reduced the top corporate tax rate from 35 percent to 24 percent.

The tax reform provisions of the bill have had minimal support. As a result, further discussion of repealing the tax deferral on overseas profits has been limited.

The Bring Jobs Home Act (S.2884/H.R.5542) would have provided businesses a tax credit equal to 20 percent of the cost of moving overseas jobs back to the United States.

It would also have ended tax deductions and loopholes for companies that ship jobs overseas.

Under present law, the cost of moving a company's employees to a new location is defined as a business expense that qualifies for a tax break.

Despite support from over 130 co-sponsors, the bill was voted down in the House in June 2012.

Currency Manipulation

The aspect of potential trade reform with by far the most bipartisan support has been currency reform, specifically with respect to China.

The Currency Reform for Fair Trade Act was passed by the Senate in 2011 and in June 2012 had bipartisan support in the House with 233 co-sponsors in both parties.

While the number of co-sponsors was enough to pass the legislation in the House, the Republican leadership blocked submission of the bill for a vote.

Interestingly enough, the bill was not supported by President Obama and was opposed by Treasury Secretary Geithner.

Here again we see the globalist orientation of the President and Secretary Geithner, in which minimizing disruptions of existing trade imbalances is given priority over protecting U.S. manufacturing.

A study by the Economic Policy Institute (EPI) found the U.S. lost 2.8 million jobs between 2001 and 2010 that were directly attributed to the trade deficit with China.

The study also identified China's currency manipulation as a principle cause of U.S. job loss.

The EPI has previously reported U.S. job loss of more than 680,000 due to NAFTA, and now estimates the U.S. will lose another 159,000 jobs from the recent agreement with Korea.

The agreements with Columbia and Panama undermine U.S. job growth and facilitate tax evasion through offshore bank accounts for corporations and the wealthy.

Tax Reform
Conservative criticism of Republicans' refusal to accept tax increases has revealed divisions in the party over how to deal with the deficit.

Bruce Bartlett held senior policy roles in the Reagan and George H.W. Bush administrations and was also a staff advisor to Representatives Jack Kemp and Ron Paul.

In a recent book on tax reform Bartlett analyzes the impact of the George W. Bush tax cuts, compared to projections by the Congressional Budget Office (CBO).

In 2001 the CBO projected a cumulative surplus of $3.5 trillion through 2008. Instead there was a cumulative deficit of $5.5 trillion.

According to the CBO, during the eight years of the Bush administration lower revenues from tax cuts increased the debt by $1.6 trillion, while slow growth reduced revenues further by $1.4 trillion.

In the same period deficit spending added another $2.4 trillion to the national debt.

Bartlett cited the failure of the Bush tax cuts to stimulate growth, and argued that allowing them to expire would raise an additional $4 trillion in revenue over the next ten years.

Bartlett has also criticized the Republican obsession with tax cuts that works to the detriment of fiscal responsibility.

Former Republican Governor Jeb Bush echoed Bartlett's concern in a June 2012 interview about the deficit.

Governor Bush said he would support a plan to reduce spending by $10 for every $1 dollar increase in revenue (opposed by all candidates in the 2012 Republican primary), and believed that both Reagan and his father, George H.W. Bush, would also have supported such a plan.

Claims that cutting taxes spur growth are not borne out by recent experience.

While taxes were raised during the Clinton administration and cut during the George W. Bush administration, GDP growth averaged 4 percent in the Clinton years and 2.7 percent during the non-recession years under Bush.

Bartlett has also insisted the conservative goal of a balanced budget is not served by what he views as fanatical adherence to cutting taxes to starve the government of revenue and thereby force reductions in spending.

Here again, government spending fell in conjunction with higher taxes under Clinton, whereas spending grew in conjunction with tax cuts under Bush.

Bartlett and Jeb Bush are not alone in criticizing what they consider extreme positions advocated by the Tea Party, exemplified by the pledge called for by lobbyist Grover Norquist to oppose any increase in taxes.

Former Arkansas Governor Mike Huckabee, Rep. Duncan Hunter (R-CA), former Republican National Committee chairman Haley Barbour, and former Sen. Chuck Hagel (R-NE) have also criticized the outright rejection of taxes to raise revenues.

In contrast, opposition to letting the Bush tax cuts expire or to any other form of tax increase was led by House Speaker John Boehner of Ohio, House majority leader Eric Cantor of Virginia, and Senate minority leader Mitch McConnell of Kentucky.

Bartlett has also ridiculed the idea the current recession is due to excessive regulation, another prominent claim made by the Republican leadership.

For example, a 2011 Wall Street Journal survey of business economists found the main obstacle to hiring was concern over a lack of demand to justify expansion.

In the context of slow consumer spending and overall low demand, Bartlett considers Republican calls for spending cuts to be sheer lunacy.

While lower spending and higher revenues will be required to balance the budget, Bartlett and others warn any significant tax increase or cuts in spending would be deflationary and put the economy at risk of even further decline.

The solution proposed by Bartlett and supported in various forms across the political spectrum is to reform the tax code and implement a value added tax (VAT).

Figure 23
U.S. Autos &
VAT Disadvantage

German Market	Made in U.S.
Price including taxes	$25,000
German VAT imposed	$4,750
Price in German market	$29,750
U.S. Producer	
VAT Disadvantage	
In German Market	$4,750

American Market	Made in Germany
Price including taxes	$25,000
German VAT rebate	-$4,750
Price in U.S. market	$20,250
U.S. Producer	
VAT Disadvantage	
In American Market	$4,750

Figure 24
10% U.S. VAT - Revenue and Incentive

	Total Imports	Total Exports	Deficit
U.S. Merchandise Trade (2014)	$2,374,101	$1,632,639	-$741,462

With U.S. 10% VAT	Total Imports	Total Exports	
	$2,374,101	$1,632,639	
	10%	10%	
VAT Tax:	$237,410		$237,410
VAT Rebate:		$163,264	$163,264
		U.S. Producer VAT incentive:	$400,674

The Value Added Tax (VAT)

A VAT system applies a tax to business sales, and provides a credit on business purchases.

A retail business would receive a credit for purchases from suppliers, and be taxed on sales to consumers. Because the consumer pays the final tax, a VAT is a tax on consumption.

The VAT is a multi-stage tax applied at each point of sale, intended to capture the value added at each stage of production.

Unique features of this kind of system make the VAT the intersection between the issue of tax reform, and the issue of unfair competition for American industry.

Most important, the systems in place around the world impose a VAT on imports, but grant a corresponding exemption for exports.

The VAT is used in over 150 countries, including all of our major trading partners.

The VAT Disadvantage

Consider taxes on passenger cars made in the U.S. and sold in Germany, compared to those made in Germany and sold in America.

Figure 23 shows an American car sold in the U.S. for $25,000 that includes taxes.

When that car is exported to Germany, it is taxed a second time by imposition of a 19 percent VAT, equal to $4,750.

The car then sells in the German market for $29,750, where it competes with a comparable German car selling for $25,000.

As a result, the U.S. producer is taxed twice and suffers a disadvantage of 19 percent in the German market.

Then consider a German car sold in Germany for $25,000 that includes taxes.

When that car is exported to the U.S., the German producer receives a VAT rebate of $4,750.

The car then sells in the American market for $20,250, where it competes with a comparable American car selling for $25,000.

So the U.S. producer also suffers a disadvantage of 19 percent in the American market.

This is why the trade deficit is a structural problem that won't be solved until the U.S. has a VAT comparable to those of our trading partners.

Figure 24 shows the goods trade deficit for 2014, and how a U.S. VAT would work.

In 2014 the goods trade deficit was over $741 billion dollars.

If the U.S. had a VAT of 10 percent, in 2014 taxes on imports would have been $237 billion.

At the same time, producers in this country would have received rebates of $163 billion on exports.

The difference ($237b - $163b) would generate $74 billion in revenue.

As important as that revenue would be, the impact on the economy would be far greater than the amount raised in taxes.

The existing export and import disadvantage for companies producing in this country would be offset by the VAT.

A U.S. VAT would tax imports but not exports, in the same way the VAT is used in over 150 countries around the world.

The result would be to create an incentive for companies to produce in this country instead of overseas.

Minimize Tax Revenue;
Maximize Tax Incentive
SWIFT Act proposals include a *refundable VAT*, because using this kind of tax would reduce the trade deficit.

A *refundable VAT* is tax neutral for individual taxpayers, because they would receive a tax credit to offset the VAT.

Implementation is discussed in detail in the Summary section that follows.

But before you read through the details, realize there has been bipartisan support for using a VAT *to raise revenue.*

In contrast, a *refundable VAT* would be tax neutral and have no impact on individual taxpayers and most businesses.

Readers should be alert to the fact that sooner or later, the need to reduce the deficit will push Congress to impose a VAT *to raise revenue.*

It is all the more imperative, therefore, for the public to get behind the idea of adopting a *refundable VAT*, which would not raise taxes on consumers.

Politicians see imposing a VAT as a way *to raise revenue* and potentially balance the federal budget.

But implementing a *refundable VAT* would reduce the trade deficit and create 15 million jobs.

Along with creating 15 million new jobs, revival of American Industry would mean we can simultaneously grow the tax base and increase the rate of economic growth overall.

Thus, faster growth and a larger tax base would generate higher tax revenues, without raising taxes.

Figure 19
Impact of Goods Trade Deficit Reduction ($Billions)
on Manufacturing Employment (Millions)

Annual Goods Deficit:

    Reduce by $400 Billion

	Direct Gain in Manufacturing Jobs	Supply Chain Employment	Re-spending Employment
	4.0	6.7	4.6

Direct Job Gain:	4.0
Supply Chain Job Gain:	6.7
Re-spending Job Gain:	4.6

Total Employment Gain:	15.3

Source: Josh Bivens, 2003. Updated Employment Multipliers for the U.S. Economy. (Washington, D.C.: Economic Policy Institute). No. 268, Table 8. Based on 1 manufacturing job for every $1.2 million of goods imports. Calculation reflects deduction in job gains from increased productivity.

Figure 24
10% U.S. VAT - Revenue and Incentive ($millions)

	Total Imports	Total Exports	Deficit
U.S. 2014 Merchandise Trade	$2,374,101	$1,632,639	-$741,462

With U.S. 10% VAT	Total Imports	Total Exports	
	$2,374,101	$1,632,639	
	10.0%	10.0%	
VAT Tax:	$237,410		$237,410
VAT Rebate:		$163,264	$163,264
		U.S. Producer	
		VAT incentive:	$400,674

Source: Merchandise Trade figures from U.S. Census Bureau.

Summary

Strategic investments funded by the federal government are an imperative for economic recovery and long term stability

As shown in Figure 19, reducing the goods trade deficit by $400 billion a year would create over 15 million new jobs.

Figure 24 shows a VAT of 10 percent would provide incentives of $400 billion a year for domestic manufacturing.

The 10 percent VAT would be fully refundable for individual tax payers.

A *refundable VAT* would be tax neutral for individual taxpayers, because they would receive a credit equivalent to the tax.

Refundable VAT:
Issues and Implementation
In 2010 the bipartisan Debt Reduction Task Force proposed comprehensive tax reform through a debt reduction plan (DRP).

The relevance of the DRP is the way the mortgage interest deduction is incorporated into the plan.

The plan would allow all taxpayers to claim a refundable credit for home mortgage interest expenses.

The credit being refundable means individuals with no tax liability would receive an equivalent tax rebate. Other filers would use the credit to reduce their taxable income.

A *refundable VAT* would work the same way, with the impact being tax neutral for individual taxpayers.

This means a 10 percent VAT on most things you buy, would be offset by a 10 percent tax credit.

The refundable credit would only apply to things that are taxable under a VAT, which for example would not include mortgage interest or medical expenses.

The same Congress that would have no problem imposing a VAT *to raise revenue*, is also fully capable of implementing a *refundable VAT* that raises very little revenue but would reduce the trade deficit and create millions of new jobs.

While I hope you'll agree a *refundable VAT* is the better option, don't expect the political establishment to like the idea.

Congress stands to lose a future source of revenue, while Wall Street and U.S. Multinationals with offshore production stand to lose profits.

The Wall Street / Trade complex and its allies in Washington will do everything possible to stop a *refundable VAT* from passing in Congress.

Figure 25

SWIFT Act Investment

11 Year Revenue Projections ($Billions)

0.5% Financial Transactions Tax (FTT) $2,198

10% Value Added Tax (VAT) $899

=========

Total $3,097

VAT revenue based on Debt Reduction Taskforce (2010), Restoring America's Future:
Reviving the Economy, Cutting Spending and Debt, and Creating a Simple, Pro-Growth
Tax System, (Washington, D.C., Bipartisan Policy Center), page 124. Figures shown
reflect deduction for VAT refunded to individual taxpayers. FTT revenue based on 50%
reduction in trading volume and 1% of GDP at 2% rate of growth.

Impact on Business

A VAT would also be tax neutral for most businesses, because the VAT would be included in their sales.

What matters is that a VAT system would impose a 10 percent tax on imports, while exports would receive a rebate equivalent to the 10 percent tax.

The effect would create incentive for domestic production, as exporting would become more profitable than importing.

Impact on Government

In 2014 a 10 percent VAT on imports would have generated $237 billion in revenue.

In the same year, a 10 percent tax credit applied to exports would have generated $163 billion in rebates.

The difference ($237b - $163b) would have generated $74 billion in revenue.

But over time, the value of imports would go down, and so would the revenue generated by the VAT.

The *refundable VAT* paid by consumers would be revenue neutral for the government, because individuals would receive a credit equivalent to the tax.

Overall, implementing a *refundable VAT* would mean the federal government, over an 11 year period, might only retain some $900 billion in VAT revenue.

Financial Transactions Tax (FTT)

A financial transactions tax of 0.5 percent (one half of one percent) would raise an additional $2.2 trillion over 11 years to fund investments in new technologies we need for long term growth.

An FTT would not only offset the cost involved, but would also help reduce speculation and establish greater parity between the returns made on financial investments and those made in manufacturing.

It makes no sense to complain about distortions caused by the financial sector when financial investment is far more profitable than investment n productive industry.

Figure 25 shows VAT and FTT revenues combined could generate $3 trillion over 11 years for investments in manufacturing and high technology industries.

If we are serious about long term recovery, we have to give serious consideration to what steps we need to take.

The current trajectory is suicidal.

The economy is bleeding to death, and stimulus for consumption is no longer a viable option.

We owe $19 trillion dollars, but thanks to offshoring we don't have the tax base required to pay down the debt.

We can bring back American industry, or we can look forward to a time when the national economy looks like that of Detroit.

Ultimately, communities that lose their tax base go bankrupt.

Thanks to offshoring, this country's manufacturing base has been sent overseas.

Both the value added and the jobs associated with that production have been lost.

These are the issues that any serous plan for recovery has to address.

But investing $1 trillion dollars in clean engine technology and other alternative energy would easily cut oil imports in half, equivalent to a 20 percent reduction in the total deficit in goods.

The overall result would be lower unemployment and stronger growth that would make the American market that much more attractive for domestic investment.

Over time the effects of investment would snow ball, creating more and more incentive favoring domestic production over offshoring.

Using wage standards to create markets and using a VAT to reduce the trade deficit are also critical to creating millions of new jobs.

Taken together, this set of proposals is a comprehensive plan that provides a road map to permanent recovery.

Economic Restructuring

The Obama administration does not fully appreciate the necessity of changing the structure of the economy.

SWIFT Act proposals address three critical areas of structural reform that are no longer an option.

I. Strategic Investment
- Alternative energy
  Wind energy
  Solar energy
  Biofuels
  Clean engine technology
- Nanotechnology
- Advanced manufacturing

II. Financial Reform
- Break up the banks
- Regulate derivatives and repeal exemptions
- Prohibit granting of stock options to corporate executives
- Establish a voluntary private employee pension plan, administered by the CFPB.
- Repeal the Citizens United decision that allows unlimited campaign contributions

III. Trade & Tax Reform
- Impose wage standards on imports
- Tax financial transactions
- Pass a *refundable VAT*

The Obama administration has provided funding for strategic investments, with the exception of clean engine technology.

There are two issues.

First, as commendable as the president's strategic investment policy has been, it doesn't come close to being adequate.

Second, in the run up to the 2012 election, the president was criticized for spending $90 billion over two years on a wide range of programs.

But we need spending of $300 billion a year, with three quarters of that allocated to advanced technology investments.

A financial transactions tax should be implemented without delay.

Strategic investments should be implemented without delay.

The *refundable VAT* should be phased in over a 3 year period, to ensure the impact isn't contractive.

Being liberal or conservative is not the issue.

We can make these investments, or we can live with the consequences of stagnation and decline.

The Politics of VAT

The proposal to implement a *refundable VAT* does not require changing the current tax system.

That means there is no reason for politicians to stall.

There is no reason for members of Congress to delay adopting the plan with endless talk about tax reform, which has no timeline but will ultimately lead to higher taxes.

There is no reason a *refundable VAT* can't be passed in 2016.

The bipartisan Debt Reduction Plan (DRP) proposed *implementing a 6.5 percent VAT, along with reducing the mortgage interest deduction by 85 percent.*

Be advised, there is no time to waste.

Congress has every motivation to reduce or eliminate deductions, and impose a VAT *to raise revenue.*

We need to secure passage of a *refundable VAT* before Congress comes up with a way to use a standard VAT to raise revenue by raising taxes.

Bipartisan Consensus

The historic distinction between liberals and conservatives has been overtaken.

Today we have outright collusion between Congressional Republicans and New Democrats who support offshoring and ignore the consequences of deindustrialization that results.

While free trade is promoted by Republicans as a cornerstone of conservative principles, there are many with unquestionable conservative credentials who are vehemently opposed to unrestricted trade.

But the ruling coalition of New Democrats and Congressional Republicans promotes the globalist view that unregulated markets are the foundation of growth.

Unregulated markets have in fact spurred unprecedented growth in trade and world financial markets.

The issue lies in the composition and character of that growth, which has brought rising inequality and escalating debt in national economies, both in the developed world and in poor countries.

The result has been stagnant world demand, accompanied by the rise of multinational companies and global financial markets that undermine sovereignty and national economies all over the world.

Meanwhile, we're subjected to 24/7 news coverage of the liberal / conservative divide between Democrats and Republicans, which makes no mention of bipartisan support for the Wall Street view of world development.

Those who fall victim to this charade have succumbed to the politics of distraction, and waste their energies by barking up the wrong tree.

Globalism as ideology is not inherently liberal or conservative, but has been adopted by both parties as the cornerstone of economic policy.

The result has been an on-going corruption of our politics.

Reform will require heightened awareness among the public and a willingness to participate in an historic movement of political opposition.

If the public is not willing, there will be no chance to overcome the ruling coalition of New Democrats and Congressional Republicans who control government policy.

Actions Speak Louder Than Words

President Obama was the leading proponent of recent trade agreements and the proposed Trans Pacific Partnership.

As we've seen, the benefits of the export side are used to justify those agreements, while job loss from the trade deficit is ignored.

Getting a clear picture of where the president stands is also made difficult by his conflicting positions on a range of issues.

For example, the administration has requested an increase in the budget for the Commodity Futures Trading Commission (CFTC) to $322 million.

Under Dodd-Frank the CFTC has oversight responsibility for some $300 trillion in previously unregulated markets for domestic swaps (a form of derivative), in addition to its original oversight of the commodity futures market.

With a staff of around 700, the CFTC is tiny in comparison to other regulatory agencies.

For example, the Office of the Comptroller of the Currency (OCC) has a budget of $3 billion a year and nearly 4,000 employees.

Along with Treasury Secretary Geithner, the OCC has been at the center of recent controversy over exemptions from Dodd-Frank regulations.

Julie Williams, chief counsel for the OCC, has insisted the Volcker rule restricting proprietary trading is unnecessary, because that kind of trading was not what caused the financial crisis.

In fact, the Senate Subcommittee on Investigations issued a report describing how proprietary trading "led to dramatic losses in the case of Deutsche Bank and undisclosed conflicts of interest at Goldman Sachs."

Volcker himself expressed concern that Williams was trying to weaken the Dodd-Frank provision, but was criticized by OCC head John Walsh for raising the issue.

Along the same lines, Treasury Secretary Geithner's exemption for FOREX trades could provide a way for banks to structure non-currency trades to fit the definition of a foreign exchange swap, which would thereby qualify for the exemption.

In October 2012 Secretary Geithner was again called to testify before Congress, this time regarding the infamous LIBOR scandal.

LIBOR (London Interbank Offered Rate) is the most widely used financial index in the world.

Geithner knew the index was rigged as early as 2007, and while he notified British authorities in 2008, there was nothing revealed to the public about what was going on.

There is clear evidence that traders at the largest banks were actively engaged in rigging the index between 2005 and 2008.

Geithner was president of the New York Federal Reserve at the time.

Along with 10-year Treasury notes and the Fed funds rate, the CFTC estimates over $800 trillion of financial instruments are pegged to the LIBOR, including $350 trillion in derivatives.

If the rate was manipulated by 10 basis points over 5 years, the result would be $4 trillion in fraudulent transactions.

Business journalist Aaron Task makes the analogy that the LIBOR scandal is like discovering the Dow Jones or the S&P 500 is rigged.

David Kotok, Chief Investment Officer for Cumberland Advisors, made a similar assessment by saying the discovery was like finding out Greenwich Mean Time isn't really accurate.

Jim Rickards, a partner at JAC Capital Advisors, has said Geithner could face "criminal liability" for failing to refer LIBOR manipulation to the FBI or the Justice Department.

According to Rickards, "A fraud is a crime. You can't witness a crime and not call the cops. Geithner might be guilty of aiding and abetting a crime."

But House member Peter King (R – New York) describes Geithner as "the classic example of someone who has a constituency of one: He has the president."

So the question that arises is why the president would choose to protect Geithner when there should be no argument that his responsibility is to protect the public.

Wall Street banks were caught dealing off the bottom of the deck.

Geithner's reaction appears to have been along the lines of well, the Federal Reserve deals off the bottom of the deck, so why shouldn't Wall Street banks?

A recent book, *Confidence Men*, describes early administration policy sessions in which Geithner warned the president that prosecuting financial crimes could undermine public confidence in the system.

If that's true, the president may have made the political calculation that maintaining stability was more important than launching criminal investigations on Wall Street.

But an old adage says we are judged by the company we keep. Was Geithner the best the president could do?

The record for both houses of Congress, regulatory agencies, the SEC, Treasury, and the President's support for Geithner, points to a Wall Street agenda that is both bipartisan and deeply corrupt.

The facts are shocking and outright disgusting. Senator Bernie Sanders (I-Vermont) sponsored a petition drive to have Geithner removed from office.

While more than 230,000 people signed it, there was no sign the president so much as flinched.

More than a few observers have noted the Democrats used to rely on campaign contributions from unions.

But now we have New corporate Democrats who make up a moderate, pro-business party that corporations and Wall Street have no need to fear.

Consider for example the controversy over Obama's Secretary of Agriculture, Tom Vilsack.

Vilsack has been called a shill for his former employer, Monsanto, evidenced by his recent ruling to exempt genetically modified (GM) alfalfa from regulation.

GM alfalfa is known to cross-pollinate, so that there is no protection for organic varieties from ultimate contamination with GM strands of the crop.

Despite enormous protest from organic farmers, the administration has been silent on the issue.

Even Bruce Bartlett, former chief economist in the Reagan administration, has described Obama as a centrist.

In an interview with Chris Matthews, Bartlett said "The dirty secret is that Obama is a moderate conservative. If I were a liberal, I probably would be upset."

The Wall Street / Trade Complex
As the volume of world trade has tripled since the late 1990s, the profits of U.S. multinationals and Wall Street banks have soared.

Corporate offshoring and the growth of financial profits are two sides of the same coin.

While corporate profits are at record levels thanks to offshoring, world financial assets have grown at 3 times the rate of world GDP.

What is called free trade is more accurately understood as a Wall Street con game.

Trade describes selling U.S. products to other countries, and vice versa.

Offshoring entails shutting down U.S. factories, re-building production centers in China, and selling those made-in-China products in the American market.

Offshoring is not trade, but rather a Wall Street con game that links profits from low wage labor to higher stock prices.

Offshoring drives profits and higher stock prices, at the expense of American industry.

The destruction of the U.S. economy is nothing more than a footnote that helps document the process.

Offshoring and the New Economy are two sides of the same coin.

The Wall Street / Trade complex defines the terms of engagement between the U.S. and the world economy, based on low wage labor in global supply chains.

The New Economy is simply the domestic manifestation of that system.

Politics has become a process of devoting enormous energy and resources to issues on which liberals and conservatives are never likely to agree.

But offshoring provides an opportunity to form a bipartisan consensus in society that is a prerequisite for overcoming bipartisan consensus in Washington.

The untold thousands of former CEOs of U.S. based companies destroyed by outsourcing are business people, and tend to think of themselves as more conservative than liberal.

Yet Congressional Republicans support a globalist agenda that bears no resemblance to the conservative principles espoused by Paul Craig Roberts, Ross Perot, Pat Choate, Pat Buchanan, or Lou Dobbs.

It was Ross Perot who famously predicted the impact of NAFTA would be a "giant sucking sound" of U.S. industry and jobs going to Mexico.

In the run up to the 1992 election, exit polls showed 42 percent of Republicans and 33 percent of Democrats favored Perot.

A poll conducted by Time Magazine showed Perot with 37 percent, whereas President Bush and Bill Clinton were tied for second place with each having 24 percent.

While Perot's lead faded after he suspended his campaign, he subsequently re-entered the race and won just under 19 percent of the vote with 20 million votes.

That sentiment among voters hasn't gone away, but has been overshadowed by the changed orientation of the two main political parties.

Congressional Republicans and New Democrats support a globalist agenda that has nothing to do with free trade, but has everything to do with profits for Wall Street banks and U.S. companies with offshore production.

The system is rigged.

Regardless of which party wins the election, the corporate alliance with Wall Street that promotes offshoring is guaranteed victory in the Trade War.

The Wall Street / Trade complex has sided with China, and that's why the U.S. Chamber of Commerce funnels millions of dollars in campaign contributions from secret donations to promote offshoring.

True conservatives are no more represented by Congressional Republicans than true liberals are represented by New Democrats in Congress.

The problem with our economy has nothing to do with the differences between liberals and conservatives.

The problem with our economy has everything to do with bipartisan support for a globalist agenda that promotes offshoring and the deindustrialization of America.

Wall Street profits from the process and has used the IMF to promote the interests of the financial sector at the expense of economic development and responsible growth in developing countries.

Corruption of our politics by the Wall Street / Trade complex is the most critical problem we face.

Campaign ads that highlight differences between Democrats and Republicans distract our attention from bipartisan support for offshoring through trade deals.

What we need is for our politicians to recognize the problem of stock values tied to offshoring and propose the legislation we need to address it.

Economic policy issues debated between the parties only account for a fraction of the problem we face.

The overwhelming problem is Wall Street's promotion of offshoring and speculation, which is perpetuated through bipartisan consensus in Washington.

This is our problem.

Today there is no such thing as free trade.

With offshoring and global supply chains there is instead an interlocking global system that ties low wage labor to the stock market.

What we have is trade in low wage components, trade in sovereign bonds used to finance debt, and financial speculation that amounts to placing bets on the performance of national economies.

That system is a Wall Street con game, promoted as an ideology of globalism with blatant disregard for the national interest of any country or the consequences for national economies around the world.

Trade War Veterans

The army of the unemployed is not a volunteer army. People's lives have been shattered, through no fault of their own.

The country has been deeply wounded, and the economy is bleeding to death.

We don't have to give in to the idea that it's all so complicated and overwhelming, that there's nothing we can do.

That is precisely what the second most powerful alliance on earth wants you to think.

The second most powerful alliance on earth is the Wall Street / Trade complex, backed by bipartisan support in Washington for unrestricted trade and unregulated finance.

But there is something we can do, because we are in fact, the 99 percent.

We have the power to mobilize and change the system. We can join together and form the most powerful alliance the world has ever seen.

The question today isn't whether we have that power, but only whether we refuse to accept the corruption of our politics and rise up to reform the system.

If we fail to summon the courage of our convictions and insist on believing in ourselves, we will forfeit the future to those who see privilege and abuse of power as a means to an end.

The end they seek is nothing less than to steal the wealth of this country, and steal the wealth of the entire world, from all of us who work throughout our lives to build security for ourselves and our families.

The only way to stop them is to look around and see the rigged game of politics for what it has become.

We have to wake up.

Like so many Americans before us, we have to take a stand, and defend our hard won liberty.

Bipartisan support for offshoring exemplifies the political movement toward globalism.

If that support is to be overcome, the opposition will have to become fully bipartisan as well.

The Republican leadership in Congress reflects the party's move toward globalism, and is completely at odds with conservatives who think we should put America first.

There is certainly strong support from conservatives in recent bipartisan calls to break up the banks.

Even the Wall Street Journal has published editorials that support the idea of a financial transactions tax.

Breaking up the banks and imposing an FTT are critical reforms needed to end speculation and restore stability to the financial system.

While Pat Buchanan and others support the use of tariffs, using a VAT to reform the tax code would achieve the same end by taxing imports and using the revenue to subsidize exports.

Imposing wage standards on imports will both protect U.S. industry and create consumer markets overseas for American products.

There is ample common cause for a bipartisan alliance to reverse the decline of our economy and restore American manufacturing to a position of dominance that is the envy of the world.

Effective opposition to the globalist alliance in Washington will require widespread support for a united front that can mobilize the public and force the passage of meaningful reform.

Toward that end, we need to appreciate the distinction between the level of government spending, and what kind of spending is involved.

The reality is that government spending works to stimulate the economy. In the context of recession, lower spending would bring deflation.

This is the danger posed by austerity and why simply reducing the size of government won't bring good results.

There are too many examples to ignore, in the developing world and now in Europe as well.

But the level of spending is a very different issue than the question of how government spending should be allocated.

Government investment is critical to lay the foundation for U.S. dominance in the new industrial revolution that is coming and is already well underway.

When manufacturing has been revived as the fundamental driver of value added growth and the trade deficit has been eliminated, the economy will be restored to historic growth rates and a larger tax base that can support permanent recovery.

Until then we should support the necessary spending on strategic investments, and oppose the outright collusion between Congress, Wall Street, and U.S. multinationals with offshore production.

Stopping the leakage in demand and investment from imports and speculation requires meaningful reform of both finance and trade.

Any program of permanent recovery will have to address these twin sources of economic leakage in order to succeed.

We Can Change Our Minds
If we act out of fear, we will perish.

Political discussion centers on spending cuts, because we're afraid of the budget deficit.

But the trade deficit is infinitely more important, because it undermines domestic production and thereby undermines the economy's capacity to create wealth and jobs.

Political discussion centers on tax cuts, because we're afraid of taxes.

Yet passing a value added tax (VAT) is a critical measure we need to tax imports so we can use the revenue to fund strategic investments in manufacturing.

The Federal Reserve's fear of inflation led to engineering slow growth and credit booms that ended in the 2008 financial crisis.

The result today is that the economy has been stripped of productive capacity and left at a virtual standstill.

Consumers fear rising prices, without realizing the cost of cheap imports is job loss.

But most of us can't afford to buy anything without a job.

We know what's wrong with the economy, and why our politicians aren't likely to fix it.

We have the diagnosis. You're holding it in your hands.

We can turn the economy around, save ourselves, and save our country for future generations to come.

But we have to change our minds about what's acceptable and what isn't.

We have to decide that we won't accept child labor and low wage imports that have destroyed our lives, our economy, and our prospects for the future.

We have to decide that we won't accept Wall Street speculation that cost us taxpayers trillions of dollars and today still threatens the entire financial system with collapse.

Most important, we have to make the decision to change the system.

If you think you're ready, please visit the website at swiftact.com, and sign the petition to support SWIFT Act legislation.

Sources

Wall Street, Trade, and the New Economy

Figure 1 – *Wall Street, Trade, and the New Economy*, Vol. 2, Figure 2: 11.
Figure 3: Ibid, Vol. 3, Figure 17:73.
Figure 4: Ibid, Vol. 3, Figure 18:73.
Figure 5: Ibid, Vol. 3, Figure 4:10.
Figure 6: Ibid, Vol. 3, Figure 5:10.

Smart Growth

Material is excerpted from *Wall Street, Trade, and the New Economy*, Volumes 1-3.
Figure 7: *Wall Street, Trade, and the New Economy*, Vol. 2, Figure 3: 10.
Figure 8: Ibid, Vol. 2, Figure 4:10.
Figure 9: Ibid, Vol. 2, Figure 7:11.
Figure 10: Ibid, Vol. 1, Figure 5: 20.
Figure 11: Ibid, Vol. 2, Figure 8:12.
Figure 12: Ibid, Vol. 2, Figure 9:13.
Figure 13: Ibid, Vol. 2, Figure 10:14.
Figure 14: Ibid, Vol. 2, Figure 11:15.
Figure 15: Ibid, Vol. 3, Figure 15:72.
Figure 16: Ibid, Vol. 3, Figure 16:72.

Wage Standards

Richard Duncan, 2005. *The Dollar Crisis: Causes, Consequences, Cures* (New York: John Wiley and Sons).

Industrial Policy

Robert Pollin and Dean Baker, 2009. *Public Investment, Industrial Policy, and U.S. Economic Renewal*, (Amherst: Center for Economic and Policy Research), Working Paper Series 211, December.

Laura D'Andrea Tyson, 2012. "Why Manufacturing Still Matters," Economix.blogs.nytimes.com, February 10, 2012.

Vaclav Smil, "The Manufacturing of Decline," (Breakthrough Journal, Summer, 2011).

Dani Rodrik, "Industrial Policy for the Twenty-First Century," Unpublished paper (Cambridge: John F. Kennedy School of Government, September 2004).

Gregory Tassey, 2011. *Beyond the Business Cycle: The Need for a Technology-Based Growth Strategy*, (Washington, D.C.: National Institute of Standards and Technology), December.

Marc Fasteau, "Industrial Policy Reconsidered," huffingtonpost.com, December 17, 2011.

Ernest F. Hollings, "Industrial Policy," economyincrisis.org, March 13, 2012.

Michael Lind, "Who's Afraid of Industrial Policy?," salon.com, January 31, 2012.

Clyde Prestowitz, "U.S. Industrial Policy Neglects Manufacturing," journalgazette.net, March 12, 2012.

Breakthrough Institute, *Where Good Technologies Come From: Case Studies in American Innovation*, (Washington, D.C.: Breakthrough Institute, December 2010).

Gary Pisano and Willy Shih, 2009. "Restoring American Competitiveness," in *Harvard Business Review* 87, Nos. 7-8 (July-August).

Alan Tonelson, 2012. "The Manufacturing Slowdown Continues." Economyincrisis.org, June 22, 2012.

Michele Nash-Hoff, "American Manufacturing Has Declined More than Most Experts Have Thought," HuffingtonPost.com, March 28, 2012.

Financial Reform

Glass-Steagall Act
Addicting Info, 2012. "Newt Gingrich Calls for Reinstating Glass-Steagall, Admits Deregulating Banking Industry Was a Mistake," addictinginfo.org, November 16, 2012.

Bloomberg, "U.S. Senators Propose Reinstating Glass-Steagall Act (Update 3)," Bloomberg.com, December 16, 2009.

Alexander Bolton, "Senate Democrats not with Warren on reinstating Glass-Steagall bank act." TheHill.com, May 31, 2012.

Harvey Gold, "Forget Dodd-Frank: Reinstate Glass Steagall." Hg.scimth.net, March 1, 2012.

Jason Linkins, "McCain, Cantwell Battle the Monolith to Reinstate Glass-Steagall," huffingtonpost.com, March 18, 2010 and May 25, 2011).

Maurice Hinchey, (Congressman). "Hinchey Reintroduces Bill to Reinstate Glass-Steagall Act; Break Up MegaBanks that Caused Financial Crisis." Hinchey.house.gov. July 7, 2011.

Shira Schoenberg, "Elizabeth Warren would reinstate Glass-Steagall Act in response to J.P. Morgan loss." Blog.masslive.com, May 15, 2012.

Alex Seitz-Wald, "Paul Ryan: 'I Agree' We Need To Reinstate Glass-Steagall," thinkprogress.org, November 9, 2011.

Jeffrey Steinberg, "Time to Reinstate Glass-Steagall." housingpredictor.com, June 16, 2012.

Nancy Spannaus, "Toward a Mass Mobilization to Restore Glass-Steagall," EIR, June 24, 2011.

Vekshin, Alison. "U.S. Senators Propose Reinstating Glass-Steagall Act (Update 3)." Bloomberg.com, December 16, 2009.

Vermont Public Radio, "Could Glass-Steagall Have Stopped JPMorgan Loss?" Vpr.net/npr/153095800, May 21, 2012.

Luigi Zingales, "Why I was won over by Glass-Steagall," ft.com, June 10, 2012.

Breaking Up Banks
Federal Reserve Bank of Dallas, *Choosing the Road to Prosperity: Why We Must End Too Big to Fail – Now*, (Dallas: Federal Reserve Bank, 2011 Annual Report).

Thomas I. Palley, "Asset-based Reserve Requirements: Reasserting Domestic Monetary Control in an Era of Financial Innovation and Instability," *Review of Political Economy*, Vol. 16, No. 1, pp. 43-58, January 2004.

Thomas I. Palley, "Asset Price Bubbles and the Case for Asset-Based Reserve Requirements," *Challenge*, Vol. 46, no. 3, May/June 2003, pp. 1-21.

Quote on Bank for International Settlements: Carroll Quiqley, 1966. *Tragedy and Hope* (New York: Macmillan Company), page 324.

Financial Transaction Taxes
Stephany Griffith-Jones and Avinash Persaud, "Financial Transaction Taxes," policydialogue.org, accessed 2/10/2016.

Dean Baker, "Supercommittee of the One Percent Won't Even Think of Taxing Wall Street." Truthout.org, October 31, 2011.

Dean Baker, "The Supercommittee Should Go Really Big and Turn Against the One Percent." Truthout.org, November 21, 2011.

Dean Baker and Helene Jorgensen. "The Relationship between Financial Transactions Costs and Economic Growth." (Washington, D.C.: Center For Economic and Policy Research, 2012).

Rebecca Christie, "EU Proposes $78 Billion-a-Year Financial Transaction Tax to Start in 2014." Bloomberg.com, September 28, 2011.

National Nurses United. "What is the Wall Street Transaction Tax?" Nationalnursesunited.org.

Bill Barclay. "A Financial Transaction Tax: Revenue Potential and Economic Impact." Working Paper, (Chicago: Chicago Political Economy Group, 2010).

Center for Economic and Policy Research, "Facts and Myths About a Financial Speculation Tax," (Washington, D.C.: CEPR, December 2011).

Philippe Douste-Blazy, "To Ease the Crisis, Tax Financial Transactions," nytimes.com, September 28, 2011.

Barcelona Graduate School of Economics, "The Tobin Tax," fairobserver.com, May 2, 2012.

Robert Kuttner, "Time for a Financial Transaction Tax," americanprospect.org, May 21, 2012.

Financial Reform - Further Reading
Pam Martens and Russ Martens, 2015. "Evidence Grows Showing Wall Street as a Negative Economic Force," wallstreetonparade.com, January 27, 2015. Accessed 2/4/2015. By far the best summary chronology is shown in the lengthy quotation below:

"Just seven years after the Nasdaq crash (in 2000), Wall Street collapsed the entire U.S. financial system and the nation's economy. We are now entering the second leg of that economic collapse as deflation takes root in major industrialized nations around the globe, supply gluts proliferate on weak demand, and oil and industrial commodity prices collapse;

Wall Street brought us to the brink in 2008 through a corrupt system whose only function was to enrich its players at the nation's expense. These are a few of the milestones in that journey;

Wall Street had insider knowledge that subprime loans were going to take down the housing market because Wall Street incentivized their employees to approve loans to people who were lying about their income and could not afford the mortgage payment;

After Wall Street created the bad mortgage loans, they sold loans they knew to be likely to default to Fannie Mae and Freddie Mac, having good reason to believe those firms would fail as a result;

Wall Street created Collateralized Debt Obligations (CDOs) because it could bury its exorbitant fees inside their complexities and bundle up all of its bad loans and sell them off to unwary pension funds and institutional investors;

The rating agencies entrusted with the critical role of providing honest ratings of these CDOs were corrupted by being paid for the ratings by the Wall Street firms. This pay to play system remains in place;

Wall Street had insider knowledge that many of these CDOs were ticking time bombs. To profit from this knowledge, Wall Street firms bought Credit Default Swaps on the CDOs, a form of insurance that would pay off when the CDO defaulted or rise in value as the credit worthiness of the CDO declined. AIG sold this insurance through its AIG Financial Products division. When AIG failed, the U.S. government paid 100 cents on the dollar to Wall Street firms for the Credit Default Swaps they had purchased from AIG;

Wall Street looked around for other suckers to fleece – public school districts, towns, counties, cities and states. It knew that it was only a matter of time before its massive issuance of mortgages to people who could not afford them would blow up the housing market and create a long-term downturn, bringing rates to record lows, so it sold tens of billions of dollars of interest rate swaps to these public entities. The public entities would receive a variable rate tied to Libor; Wall Street would receive a higher, fixed rate. Wall Street then proceeded to engage in a conspiracy to rig the Libor interest rate to its advantage. Typically, the public entity ended up receiving a fraction of one percent in interest, while contractually bound to pay Wall Street firms as much as 3 to 6 percent in a fixed rate for twenty years or longer. To get out of the deals, public entities have been forced to pay Wall Street tens of billions of dollars in termination fees, further fleecing the public purse.

Wall Street's overarching function today is that of an institutionalized wealth transfer mechanism, propped up by compromised regulators and a dysfunctional Congress. As the PBS program *Frontline* reported in 2013, if your work career spans 50 years and you receive the historic return of 7 percent on stocks in your 401(k) plan, the 2 percent typical fee charged by Wall Street mutual funds will gobble up almost two-thirds of your account.

The *Frontline* program was called "The Retirement Gamble." Wall Street On Parade checked the math and found this was not a gamble but a certainty: "under a 2 percent 401(k) fee structure, almost two-thirds of your working life will go toward paying obscene compensation to Wall Street; a little over one-third will benefit your family – and that's before paying taxes on withdrawals to Uncle Sam."

All of these examples cited above are part and parcel of why the United States has the fourth most unequal income distribution in the developed world.

That income inequality, according to the Organisation for Economic Co-Operation and Development (OECD) is dampening growth prospects. The OECD found in a study released in September of 2014 that "countries where income inequality is decreasing grow faster than those with rising inequality." The study noted that in Italy, the U.K. and the United States, "the cumulative growth rate would have been six to nine percentage points higher had income disparities not widened."

The above summary indictment was excerpted from the above referenced article published online. I consider wallstreetonparade.com to be the pre-eminent online source covering Wall Street, the Federal Reserve, and Central Banks around the world.

Trade and Tax Reform

Value Added Tax (VAT)
Eric Toder, Jim Nunns, and Joseph Rosenberg, 2012. "Using a VAT to Reform the Income Tax," (Washington, D.C.: Tax Policy Center, Pew Fiscal Analysis Initiative," January 2012.

Ron Baiman, "Toward a New Political Economy for the U.S., Center for Tax and Budget Accountability," Chicago Political Economy Group, CPEG Working Paper 2010-1, January 15, 2010.

Ron Baiman, "What we need to do to Revive our Economy," CPEG online

Michael Graetz, "VAT as the Key to Real Tax Reform," Tax Analysts 2011.

Robert S. McIntyre, Matthew Gardner, Rebecca J. Wilkins, and Richard Phillips, *Corporate Taxpayers & Corporate Tax Dodgers 2008-10*, Citizens for Tax Justice & The Institute on Taxation and Economic Policy, (Washington, D.C.: November 2011).

Robert D. Atkinson, 2009 "Effective Corporate Tax Reform in the Global Innovation Economy," *Information and Technology & Innovation Foundation*, July 2009: 9-16

Ron Baiman, *The Linkage Between the Three Types of National Economic Deficits*, (Chicago: Chicago Political Economy Group), June 22, 2010.

Ron Baiman, "Eisenhower Era Income Tax Rates on the Upper 10% of Families Would Immediately Erase the Federal Deficit," Chicago Political Economy Group, CPEG Working Paper 2011-2, January 15, 2010.

Edward J. Kane, "The Inevitability of Shadowy Banking," Paper presented at the Federal Reserve Bank of Atlanta, 2012 Financial Markets Conference, Atlanta, GA, April 10, 2012.

Bruce Bartlett, "Are Taxes in the U.S. High or Low?," Today's Economist, May 31, 2011.

Salam Reihan "Revisiting Michael Graetz's Competitive Tax Plan," (National Review Online, 2012).

Michael Lind, 2012. "A Radical Tax Solution," Salon.com, April 24, 2012.

Chuck Marr and Brian Highsmith, 2012. *Six Tests for Corporate Tax Reform*, (Washington, D.C.: Center on Budget and Policy Priorities, 2012).

David Kocieniewski, "U.S. Business Has High Tax Rates but Pays Less," (New York: New York Times, May 2, 2011).

Further Reading
Jesse Eisinger and Jake Bernstein, "From Dodd-Frank to Dud: How Financial Reform May be Going Wrong," Propublica.org, June 11, 2012).

Bruce Bartlett, "Rich Nontaxpayers." Economix.blogs.nytimes.com, June 5, 2012.

--------, "Are We About to Repeat the Mistakes of 1937?" Economix.blogs.nytimes.com, July 12, 2011.

--------, "Misrepresentations, Regulations, and Jobs." Economix.blogs.nytimes.com, October 4, 2011.

--------, "What Role Should the Fed Follow?" Economix.blogs.nytimes.com, May 15, 2012.

--------, "Why the GOP should stop invoking Reaganomics." Washingtonpost.com, February 3, 2012.

--------, "Why Ronald Reagan Would Not Lead Today's GOP." Thefinancialtimes.com, June 15,

Pat Garofalo, 'House Republicans Serve the Banks by Voting to Repeal Key Anti-Bailout Provisions," Thinkprogress.org, June 11, 2012.

Jim Rutenberg, "Jeb Bush Questions G.O.P.'Shift to the Right." nytimes.com, June 11, 2012.

Reader Notes

Reader Notes

Reader Notes

About the Author

I taught political science for five years and received my doctorate from Tulane in 1992. After 20 years in the private sector, my reaction to the Occupy Wall Street movement was to write a series of books and establish the non-profit SWIFT Act Alliance.

The U.S. economy is in crisis, and unprecedented numbers of voters are rejecting the status quo. I wrote these books in the hope of providing a common sense guide to understanding how economies work and why ours no longer functions the way it should.

My goal is to empower readers through explanations that build economic literacy and provide clear discussion of fundamentals that led to the Great Depression and continue today in the Great Recession.

Millions of people realize we can no longer trust the establishment to manage the economy. That means the public will need greater understanding of economic fundamentals to support demands for meaningful reform.

Toward that end, SWIFT Act proposals are intended as a blueprint for what I consider to be essential aspects of reform we need for long term recovery.